It looks like love. It feels like love.
But is it love?

LOVE
AND ITS
COUNTERFEITS

by Barbara Cook

(Aglow Publications

A Ministry of Women's Aglow Fellowship, Int'l.
P.O. Box 1548
Lynnwood, WA 98046-1558
USA

Cover design by Ray Braun

Unless otherwise noted, all scripture quotations in this publication are from the Holy Bible, New International Version. Copyright 1973, 1978, 1984, International Bible Society. Other version is abbreviated as follows: KJV (King James Version).

ISBN 0-932305-78-4

Acknowledgements

I would like to express gratitude to the numerous men and women who have shared their stories and experiences with me, sometimes painful ones. Special care has been taken to guard their privacy. Their identities have been protected by the alteration of nonessential details and use of fictitious names. In some places, a composite of several similar experiences or individuals was used. Although I cannot acknowledge these persons by name, I sincerely appreciate the contribution they have made, not only to this book, but to my own life and personal growth. I am certain that each one will be happy to see others helped by their experiences and the truths discovered in our mutual attempts to meet the challenges presented by those experiences.

Contents

Introduction

I've written this book for the woman who wants to grow in her love maturity. When we grow in love, we must often let go of old habits and sometimes, old beliefs and misconceptions about love. A growth spurt is often stimulated by a painful experience, such as rejection from a loved one, disappointment in a relationship, or simple frustration as you attempt to do the right things for your children.

This book is for you if you ever wonder about the difference between emotions and love. Or question what is normal and abnormal or real and unreal. When does love call for self-sacrifice, and when does it call for an end to self-sacrifice? What about love and dependency, love and control, love and obsession, or love and romance? How do you know if what you're feeling is not love at all, but some deep need inside crying out for help? Where does trust come in?

In the following pages, you'll find popular ideas about love measured against the Bible's descriptions. We developed beliefs about these things while still in our childhood. As adult women, we must examine which of our learned habits and attitudes are motivated by love, and which need to be changed because they are harmful to us or others. We can change self-defeating ways of "loving" and experience the growth spoken of in the Bible: "That your love may abound more and more in knowledge and depth of insight, so that you may be able to discern what is best" (Phil. 1:10).

1
...
Love

Emotions are wonderful. Life would be a dreary, colorless succession of events without them. But emotions are tricky, too. They can mislead us. What *feels* real may not always be what *is* real.

In no area of our lives are the emotional mine fields more surprising than the territory of love. We so associate love with warm, cozy feelings that when we have those feelings, we seldom question the relationships in which we feel them.

One morning as Jerry, my husband, and I watched cartoons with the kids, one of Daffy Duck's lines struck us as funny. So funny, it's becoming part of the family vocabulary. Fleeing (as always) from his enemies, Daffy faced the camera and exclaimed to the audience, "I don't like pain. It hurts me!"

Humans are no different. We run from things that hurt

us. Who likes pain, anyway? We go for the "feel-good" with great predictability. We hang around people who make us feel good, watch TV programs that make us laugh (or cry), eat food that pleases our taste buds, and choose music that pleases our ears. Being human, we avoid pain and pursue pleasure. Sometimes we become the victims of our pleasure. Because it *feels good*, it's hard to distinguish counterfeit love from real love.

WHEN ATTENTION MEETS A NEED

Counterfeit love serves to meet a need somewhere in our deep recesses. Suppose, for example, you are ignored, lonely, and never valued. A stranger gives you an hour of his time, listening with his full attention as you spill out your thoughts and feelings.

You experience powerful emotions. You feel relief as you express yourself. Or warmth or lifted spirits or even intense sexual passion toward the listener. Unaccustomed to the full blast of such an emotional rush, you could easily label the feelings "love."

When one of our human needs is met, we feel loved. But the feeling is not the love. Remember: the listener is a total stranger. Suppose he turns out to be selling vacuum cleaners. Now he insists you buy one. Was what you just experienced love? Or was it manipulation?

ROBIN ENDS HER LIFE

One of the saddest times in my ministry was the day I conducted Robin's funeral. Robin had put a revolver to her pretty head when the love of her life stood her up one night. I began the funeral by describing my own feelings, knowing they were likely the same emotions with which her family and friends struggled.

"Many of us here today are troubled not only by our

feelings of loss, but also of guilt. We ponder all the things we might have done to prevent this tragedy. 'Maybe if I'd . . .' or 'If only we had . . .' run through our heads. We realize we should have taken Robin's depression more seriously. The last time I talked with her was at a Sunday night get-together a month ago.

"She was happy in her job. She felt good about herself because she had completed a stop smoking program and for the first time in years had quit. Should I have shown more concern? Encouraged her to confide not only the positives in her life, but the negatives?

"I loved Robin but not enough. Or not as well as I could have. I am partially guilty. Robin chose to end her life, but all of us could have loved her better. We wish she had given us the chance. Perhaps if we'd reached out to her more, loved her more wisely, Robin could have learned to love herself more. And to value her own life enough to go on living even when disappointed."

The congregation looked relieved. The burden of guilt was something we all shared. I led the opening prayer: "Father, we loved Robin but not enough . . . or not very well. We need your forgiveness. We need you to teach us how to love better. There is so much we don't know, Lord. We're babies in the development of this skill. Help us to grow and become aware of the needs around us. Show us how to love as you love."

ROBIN'S REASON

Later, as the family said their private good-byes to Robin, I took special note of Sam, the boyfriend. (Ironically, he hadn't stood her up at all; at least not this time. He was merely delayed since he was traveling from another state to meet her.) I knew Sam had been, for seven or eight years, the absolute center of Robin's life. Wistfully and shyly she had occasionally asked me questions about love. Questions such as, "If you can't stop thinking about a guy, isn't that a sign you're really in love?" Or "Should you ask God to take away the feelings if he doesn't want you to be with a certain person?" Later, "What if God doesn't take away the feelings?"

Robin lived with Sam for a few years. Then she moved to our city; I sensed that she wanted to make a break from a destructive relationship. But despite the progress toward independence, she believed she would only be happy if Sam loved her and married her.

Not a very impressive fellow, I thought as he stood at her casket holding a bouquet of wildflowers. In terms of human measurements (which, I realize, are rarely accurate), he seemed shabby, insecure, and far less capable than the woman who had loved him. Then a flash of insight: Robin had longed for a love that did not exist! Sam was not capable of meeting her needs. He may have loved her to the limits of his abilities, but what she needed was not his to give.

FATAL DELUSIONS

Robin's "love" was a counterfeit. Her delusions about love eventually led her to end her life. She needed to understand and experience the healthy, genuine love described in the Bible. Her intense longings felt like love. But they were not love.

Her feelings of attachment could readily be mislabeled as nice Christian qualities: commitment, loyalty, perhaps even faith. But they were not; they were symptoms of a deeper need. Because of her beliefs, Robin gave Sam power over her identity, power to determine her emotions, and power to measure her value. Although he did not want it, she gave him the power of life and death.

CHERI'S MOM ENDURES

One day I listened to Cheri, a Christian girl in our college group, describe the teenage life she'd lived before she met Christ. Gone now were the drugs, wild parties, and defiant relationship with her parents. But she deeply regreted the way she'd treated her mother.

"I was awful," she confided. "I called her terrible names. Often I yelled, 'I hate you, you old @&*!!' I wish now I could take it back." She looked thoughtful. "Mom just took it. She should have slapped me full in the face the very first time I verbally abused her. But she didn't. The more I did it, the more I believed she deserved to be treated that way. Violent or not, she'd have done me a big favor if she'd stopped my filthy mouth when it first started."

Putting up with Cheri's mouth may have seemed like the expression of patience or love to this indulgent mother. But it was not love. It was very harmful to Cheri and her mom.

WHERE IS THE ABSOLUTE?

Fortunately, the Bible offers a clear description of real love. Without access to such an absolute, we would be doomed to learn about love by trial and error. Most of us don't have that many years to live! Others have had enough of trial and error in this matter of loving. We need to see where we've gone wrong in the past. We need to examine our assumptions and preconceptions, throwing them all against the word of God with confidence that its light will clear up our muddy thinking and point us in a better way.

First Corinthians 13 is not the only description of authentic love in the Bible, but it's certainly the most beautiful and the place our study begins.

If I speak in the tongues of men and of angels, but
have not love, I am only a resounding gong or a clang-
ing cymbal. If I have the gift of prophecy and can
fathom all mysteries and all knowledge, and if I have
a faith that can move mountains, but have not love, I
am nothing. If I give all I possess to the poor and surrender my body to the flames, but have not love, I
gain nothing. Love is patient, love is kind. It does not
envy, it does not boast, it is not proud. It is not rude,
it is not self-seeking, it is not easily angered, it keeps
no record of wrongs. Love does not delight in evil but
rejoices with the truth. It always protects, always
trusts, always hopes, always perseveres. Love never
fails. But where there are prophecies, they will cease;
where there are tongues, they will be stilled; where
there is knowledge, it will pass away (1 Cor. 13:1-8).

This passage tells us what genuine love does, what it
looks like, and how to recognize it. It also points out what
real love does *not* do. It lists some items that give the
appearance of love but actually may be just that—an appearance. (For example, self-sacrifice: "If I give all I possess to the poor and surrender my body to the flames. . . .")

SELF-SACRIFICE

Few people question whether self-sacrifice is love. Most
assume, in fact, that self-sacrifice is the highest and noblest evidence of love. Scripture has a different view. Self-
sacrifice is not *always* an expression of love; it can easily
be an expression of low self-worth. Or an expression of
neurotic self-punishment. Fear can motivate sacrifice, as
misguided beliefs, or numerous other motivations, none of
which qualify as love.

Many women, like Robin and Cheri's mom, are

confused by notions of what it means to love. Because of that, they end up suffering abuse and victimization. Fran marries an alcoholic for the third time; Carrie falls "in love" on the rebound again; Janice finds her new husband abusing her, just like her ex-husband did, and her father before that. If these women examined their notions about love, they could change their ways of relating.

DISAPPOINTED AND DISILLUSIONED

Many women suffer from what they believe to be the results of love. Many are disappointed and disillusioned, often to the point of suspecting anyone who says, "I love you." Some have given up on romantic love, having decided it was their naive response to men that allowed them to be charmed and then exploited.

Many women deceived about love now want to take an honest look at their own self-deception. They are ready to examine the old assumptions and mind-sets that formed their beliefs about love. This book will compare their beliefs with the Bible's definition of love.

CHANGE IS POSSIBLE

I can't count the times women have wept in my office and poured out stories of needless, intense suffering at the hands of "love." However, a counselor cannot heal the pain, restore the ability to rightly love, or transform destructive attitudes and beliefs held since childhood—no matter how often the counselor and hurting woman meet.

But God can do all those things. He watches eagerly for opportunities to heal and restore. You can experience change from the inside out.

However, many women who have not suffered in the above ways also have questions about love. They live their lives from day-to-day, seeking to grow personally and spiritually, to reach out to those in need, to care for their families responsibly, and to do what is right and good. No spectacular ups-and-downs, no movie star glamour, no stories fit for adventure books.

A SINFUL WORLD

But those in that broad category I call "average" have their problems with love, too. We were all born into a world infected with sin. Sin is a distortion of truth. A twisting of God's intentions. Centuries of human living have distorted our perceptions of love. Each of us has blind spots and ideas about love that are way off.

GROWTH IS NOT AUTOMATIC

Growth into adulthood ought to include growth into the ability to love. We do not come into this world with the capacity to love perfectly. Just as some of us are stuck in a toddler's concept of God that we should have outgrown by now, many are also stuck in a childish view of love. We have failed to allow the years to bring an expanded understanding of love.

For a child, love is simple; it is the feeling of having one's needs met. Yet if that child is to receive love, the adult had better have a more grown-up definition! Otherwise, a mother and father try to get a baby to meet their adult needs. For the children of our world, it is vital that adults practice adult love. We live in an era when married women, single women, mothers of toddlers, grandmothers, and great-grandmothers urgently need to *learn* how to love.

WELL-INTENTIONED MISTAKES

As I've experienced firsthand what the typical woman goes through in her attempts to love and be loved, I have fallen time and time again to my knees. At times, I have loved well but not wisely. At other times, I didn't even love well! Robin's tragedy represents a vivid memory of such a time.

Another suicide brought me face to face with the same kind of failure. Only after this young man's death did I learn of his struggles with homosexuality, self-hatred, and depression. He wasn't the type to call attention to himself, so although in a position to help him, I never reached out to him—at least not enough to win the level of trust he needed in a pastor before he could ask for help.

CARING TOO MUCH

At other times, I tried too hard; I was *too* helpful. Later, I discovered my efforts were viewed as an annoyance rather than a gift of love. Like many women, I have acted on my emotions of deep caring at times when actually the more loving thing would have been to pray.

I have not always clearly distinguished between love and emotions, love and possessiveness, love and my own needs, or love and control. The best I can say for myself in those embarrassing failures is that at least I tried to love.

No excuse, however, lets me off the hook if I refuse to learn from these mistakes. The worst that could come from my blunders is detached objectivity or fear of "getting involved"—a regression to conservatism out of fear I may again make a mistake.

SELF-PROTECTION

This response may be the safest route, but it will systematically carry us into total selfishness and isolation. It may give us immunity from the sins we risk by loving. But isn't self-centered isolation another kind of sin? Psychologist Larry Crabb calls it the sin of self-protection. Fearing rejection or failure, we live careful Christian lives, observing all the rules, but guarding ourselves from our own insides until we become incapable of truly loving others.

THE FEAR OF LOVING

Women who are afraid to love because they might "fall into sin" may be in greater danger than are the women we described earlier as the desperate victims of counterfeit love: the abused, mistreated, manipulated, and exploited. I admit to this tendency. At times, I have subconsciously—even consciously—made a choice to withdraw from loving.

I strongly identify with mothers who feel they cannot bear the pain of rejection from their teenage children, with church women betrayed by a confidant they believed was a friend, and with counselors so afraid of over-identification they try to feel no emotions toward their clients.

RISKS AND REALITY

Every Christian who lives long enough will inevitably pay a price for choosing the path of love. You may wonder if the price is too high. I encourage you to renew your commitment, and keep on taking the risks. But perhaps with a more realistic, more mature acceptance of those risks. And with the clarity of thought to discern between real love and counterfeit love.

I believe women want to discern between the real thing and false love. "The word of God is living and active. Sharper than any double-edged sword," penetrating into our deepest pockets of self-deception and judging, it says, "the thoughts and attitudes of the heart" (Heb. 4:12). We do have the choice of profound change. The chance to confront our own misconceptions and self-delusions about love. The option of a better way. That active, powerful agent, the Word of God, implanted into our lives, will continue the transformation of our thinking and loving long after we lay down this book.

A DEFINITION

First Corinthians 13 is a description of love but not a definition in the dictionary sense. After all, the Bible was not written as a dictionary. But its writers used a language well-suited to our purposes; that is, of understanding love as God sees it. In our language, love can mean any number of different things: we love ice cream, we love our kids, we love baseball, we love the dog, we love our husbands and we love God.

What a hodge-podge of meanings associated with one small word! How confusing to someone learning this language! Much of the time "I love" means "I enjoy" or "I feel good."

AGAPE

The Greeks used many specific words for love that made it easier to say what they really meant. The Greek word *agape* was one rarely used in the literature of New Testament times. Today, people who have never studied Greek are familiar with it simply because the writers of the New Testament used it so often to denote love. This love was a special, more-than-human-emotion kind of love. It was divine, originating in God who alone is capable of perfect love.

Eros (sexual desire, physical attraction), *storge* (family affection), and *phileo* (friendship) were the words the Greeks commonly used for love. The last two are found in the New Testament, but *agape* is used as the basic, definitive concept of love for believers. First Corinthians 13 has given the world the opportunity to see and learn of genuine love as God intends it to be; a choice that goes beyond reciprocation or human self-interest. It is a way of living, a way of treating persons in light of their value to God. It is action; it is a choice.

We see these truths about *agape* in the entire Bible. Love is not so much defined as it is described. The more you understand Scripture as a whole, the better you understand God's concept of love. Your definition grows with the years as you gain a broader frame of reference and a greater knowledge of him.

Sometimes we miss love that stares us right in the face because we are hung up on a definition that is too narrow. If it doesn't feel mushy and gushy, it can't really be love. A well-known educator observed,

A man once told me that his dog's love was the only love in his life of which he was sure. He explained, "He always greets me with enthusiasm, he is responsive to my touch, he's forgiving, and he's there when I need him. He loves me without conditions." This was quite a statement! Either the people in this man's life had fallen short of giving him the assurance he needed, or his idea of love needed redefining.

In human relationships we are seldom guaranteed such unequivocal love and we are often given to wonder whether we are in fact loved by those closest to us. Since our definitions of love are constantly changing as we learn more about giving it each day, it's not unusual that we question whether or not we are receiving it.

A wife says to a husband (or vice versa),

"Do you love me?"

"Of course," he replies.

"Why?" she presses for a more definitive answer.

"What do you mean why? I've been married to you for 20 years, haven't I?"[1]

LOVE AND NEEDS

Our definition of love is usually based on our momentary needs. What felt like love once no longer feels like love; it doesn't address this new set of needs I have developed. Basing my concept of love on whatever meets the most strongly felt need will always be a mistake. Remember our vacuum salesman who gave attention and a listening ear to the lonely housewife?

Feelings of warmth are not the essence of love, only the by-product. *Intimacy* is not synonymous with love, even though it may be a response to it. *Admiration* may stem from love, but there is a great difference between admiring a person and loving that person. Love carries on even when admiration breaks down.

ALWAYS A CHOICE

Biblical love is always a choice; never an uncontrollable seizure. It is a decision as to how I will treat another person; even the first chapters of the Old Testament make that clear. It sponsors emotions and giving and many other by-products. But first it is a choice, freely and consciously made.

Agape love recognizes the image of God in another human and values that person as God does. *Agape* love seeks the highest good of the loved one and pursues another's best interests rather than competing for one's own demands. The woman who loves as God loves does not ignore her own value or denigrate herself. She values herself in the same way God values her. Out of her own unshakable self-worth she gives, for giving of ourselves is where it all begins.

21

2
...
What Are the Counterfeits?

It feels like love, looks like love, sounds like love, and . . .

You can even find scripture verses to convince yourself it is love you are experiencing. Which is why counterfeits are so dangerous to Christians. After all, we keenly desire to be like Christ. We desire to be loving persons. We need to think of ourselves as loving, caring individuals in order to maintain self-respect.

The counterfeits addressed in this book are:

Emotional dependency   The Messiah complex
Manipulation   Possessiveness
Sexual addiction   Obsession
Victimization   Control

Others are more subtle because they are good feelings or "right" ways of relating. For example, rescuing or helping a person in trouble is normal behavior for a Christian—it's

23

what we're supposed to do. So we may not recognize times when our rescuing behavior is actually working against the highest good of the other person.

THE LOVE CHAPTER

During our twenty years of ministry, Jerry and I have performed many weddings. We include a reading of 1 Corinthians 13 in every ceremony. Whenever I use a new paraphrase or translation, I hear comments like, "Where did you get that beautiful—ah—poem, that piece you read about love?"

I usually start with verse 4, where love is described as actions and behavior that seek the highest good of another. It *is* beautiful from any translation. But the first verses of the chapter are not so lovely. They alert us to the disturbing fact that some things *appear* to be love that are not love. Fooled by appearance, we can act in ways we consider loving that are not love at all.

> If I speak in the tongues of men and of angels, but have not love, I am only a resounding gong or a clanging cymbal. If I have the gift of prophecy and can fathom all mysteries and all knowledge and if I have a faith that can move mountains, but have not love, I am nothing. If I give all I possess to the poor and surrender my body to the flames, but have not love, I gain nothing (1 Cor. 13:1-3).

Paul wrote these inspired words to the Christians in Corinth as an answer to some squabbles in their church. From earlier chapters, it appears they were playing "my gift is better than your gift." A foolish and childish competitive attitude pervaded their questions and debates about who was most spiritual.

FATHERLY CORRECTION

Paul addressed their questions and administered a fatherly dose of correction. In a nutshell, Paul told them, "Your spiritual gifts don't count two bits if you are motivated by anything other than love."

Love is what counts, he declared. Gifts will pass away because they're only for this world. Love is eternal. Three things—faith, hope, and love will last. Love is the greatest of them all. The important thing is not what others think of your gift; the important thing is whether you really loved.

So! We can perform spiritual acts while deficient in love? We can speak in the tongues of men and angels; deliver an eloquent prophetic message; demonstrate mountain-moving faith; give away everything we own including our life for Christ—and still not love!

Paul cites pretty impressive things; things that are not exactly second-rate items in the Christian value system.

This is precisely our difficulty with love. It's easy to kid ourselves when what we're doing or feeling is something we've always labeled a mark of Christian spirituality.

HONESTY IS NOT EASY

If you're like me, you may find this subject unsettling. Although it's one I often address as a public speaker, I am not always comfortable with it. Maybe it's because I'm reluctant to examine my own ways of loving. I can recognize personal instances that resemble some of these mistakes. They can make me doubt myself.

It is most unpleasant to discover that a particular accomplishment was not the result of great love after all, but the result of some misguided need. None of us like to face that sort of truth. It's easier to justify ourselves: "Well, I did the best I could," or "When you love someone as much as I do, you have no choice. I couldn't have done anything differently."

Each of us has a history in the arena of love. For some, it's a happy history, one that makes us feel good about ourselves. For others, it's painful to recall, a series of catastrophes, mistakes, delusions, and confusing nightmare-like scenes we have never quite figured out.

"So, Barbara, don't make it worse for us," you say, "by making us think about these miserable experiences again! We just want to forget them!"

Do what you must do. My intention is not to make you focus needlessly on a painful past, but if we don't deal with past unhealthy ways of "loving," they may return to haunt us. What we learn from our mistakes will help us love better in the future.

QUESTIONS TO ASK YOURSELF

If you do choose to take a look at past failures in love, it may be helpful to ask yourself some questions:

1. I enjoy the pleasure and comforting warm feelings that come from having my needs met. But did I confuse the *feelings* with love?

2. Was I operating out of a mistaken definition of love, one I now see to have been inaccurate?

3. Have I grown into a different person now, a person more capable of mature love?

4. Was I the victim of emotional or physical abuse?

5. Was I treated unfairly or with less respect than I deserved?

6. Did I allow myself to be manipulated or used, thinking it would be unloving to stand up for myself?

7. Was this a situation in which I tried to control, possess, or remake another person? Can I avoid doing that in future relationships and situations?

8. Did I give away my identity, believing love demanded it?

9. Did I give another person too much power over my life, such as the power to control my emotions or values?

10. How have I changed since then? In what ways am I now wiser and more equipped to handle a similar experience?

WARNING SIGNALS

Following are a few warning signals to alert you to a possible counterfeit love, something other than the healthy love described in the Bible:

1. *You have given another person power over your emotions.*

2. *You have given away control of your identity.*

3. *You have violated your moral standards and beliefs.*

Margret Hoeke was recently sentenced to eight years in prison in her native Germany. At fifty-one, she brought to an ignominious end her distinguished career as secretary to the president. Not just one, but five different presidents of West Germany had selected her as their secretary. Yet, Margret was convicted of treason against her country in a trial that revealed she had been spying for a Soviet agent for fifteen years.

She supplied classified military information, secret documents, and other materials that seriously damaged the foreign policies of her government. She said she did it because "I loved him."

The man she loved was, it turned out, a Soviet KGB agent who went by the name Franz Becker. As Judge Klaus Wagner sentenced Margret, he voiced the opinion that she "had been enticed into espionage by the cunning exploitation of her love for Franz Becker." She used a miniature camera hidden in her lipstick to photograph defense secrets and stored secret materials in a hollowed-out hairbrush.

LONELY AND EXPLOITED

The newspaper listed the charming Franz Becker's whereabouts as "unknown." One sad paragraph in the news item read: "Hoeke, who began working for the president's office in 1959, testified during her trial that she grew up feeling unloved by her family. She said she was single and lonely when befriended by Becker in 1968." How tragic that Margret sacrificed her moral integrity for someone who exploited her needs and misguided ideas of love!

4. *You have enabled a destructive behavior by rescuing the person from consequences he or she should be allowed to experience as the logical results of that behavior.*

5. *You have been victimized, manipulated, or used.*

A friend of ours trains and supervises students preparing to become psychologists. I sat in on one of his classes one day and listened as he addressed concerns regarding clients who become emotionally dependent on their therapists.

"Miss Green calls me every day with an emotional emergency," one student said. "She thinks I should drop everything and get to her immediately. She calls in the middle of the night. I can't even get a decent night's rest."

Another student added, "What about suicide threats? How do we deal with those? Sometimes disturbed clients threaten to take their lives if we don't rush to comfort them instantly. How can we tell, especially in those being treated for depression, whether it's a serious threat or just a ploy for attention?"

A DAILY CRISIS

The wise teacher reminded the future therapists that any

suicide threat must be taken seriously. Then he went on to the matter of emotional dependency, illustrating with a story from his own practice.

"A client who seemed highly dependent, despite my careful efforts, threatened suicide often," he said. "She managed to create some new crisis every day. One morning she called at 3:00 a.m., saying she was terribly distraught and couldn't sleep. She threatened suicide if I didn't come over immediately and comfort her. I told her I couldn't come right then, but I offered to rearrange my schedule and meet her in the office at 8:00 a.m.

"Her demands and threats persisted, so I explained, 'If you're sure you're going to attempt suicide, then I can no longer take the legal responsibility of being your therapist. I'll come, but not for a therapy appointment. I'll bring the legal release stating you are no longer in treatment with me. Once you sign it, I won't be available to you for appointments. If you change your mind about living, you'll have to find a new therapist.' "

MANIPULATION CONFRONTED

The class chuckled as they quickly deduced the choice this client made. The teacher concluded his story: "Suddenly she felt a little better. 'I'll try to make it to morning, Doctor,' she said. 'See you at eight!' "

"But wasn't that pretty risky?" asked a student.

"No riskier than the alternatives. I can never allow my clients to manipulate me. Once I do, I've stopped loving them. I can no longer give them the help they need."

Good advice for pastors, I mused. I wrote in my notebook, "When I begin responding to manipulation, I have just stopped loving."

6. *You have submitted to treatment that makes you feel worthless—treatment that ignores your value and right to*

respect.

7. *You have found yourself willing to live in denial, refusing to take a serious look at reality.*

As a Christian, you may try to equate your denial with faith. You attempt to create an ideal by "claiming" scripture promises, fasting, praying, or other religious acts.

Harald Bredesen tells of his early Christian life when he met a girl named Jane at church and became good friends with her. After time, Harald proposed, declaring his deep love and desire for her to be his wife. Kindly, Jane replied, "Why, Harald, I love you too, but only as a brother in the Lord." To his dismay, she made it clear she did not desire a romantic relationship; Jane considered herself only a friend.

GOD'S WILL

Later, Harald believed he heard from God on the subject. "Jane is the woman I have chosen to be your wife. It is my will that you two marry."

Harald approached Jane the next time he saw her at church. "God told me it was his will for us to become husband and wife."

Jane seemed unimpressed. But at Harald's insistence she agreed to pray about it. Months went by with no change in their relationship. Jane was nice to Harald but slightly aloof, giving no signals that she had decided to "obey God." She dated other men, and after about a year, appeared to be getting serious about one of them. Fred, a friend of Harald's from the same congregation, seemed to be on the verge of engagement to Jane. About the time most men in Harald's position would have given up, he "heard from God again." As he prayed that she would obey God and marry him, he was inspired to open his Bible and read from Hebrews. In Hebrews 10:35, he read, "Cast not away therefore your confidence, which hath great recompence of reward" (KJV).

KEEP BELIEVING

"Okay, God," Harald responded. "I won't cast away my confidence. I'll just keep on believing that Jane will be mine someday. I claim that promise by faith." Much encouraged, he happily marked time waiting for Jane. Even after she became engaged. Even the day he attended Fred's and Jane's wedding. "Poor Fred," Harald thought. "Must be destined to die an early death."

A few years passed, and one day a young woman asked to speak privately with Harald after church. "Harald," she began, "God showed me that you're my future husband. I wonder if he's spoken to you about it."

Shocked and uncomfortable, Harald searched for the right words. "I do love you, Ann, but only as a sister in the Lord." As kindly and quickly as possible, he made his exit.

A few weeks later, Ann approached him again admitting that she felt terribly hurt by his unenthusiastic response to her love and a bit worried about whether she had actually heard from God after all. "But I want you to know I can wait. Because God gave me this verse in Hebrews that says, 'Cast not away therefore your confidence, which hath great recompence of reward.' "

Harald immediately recognized his own delusion. Once he saw it, he could let go of his fantasy and begin to date again. Eventually, he fell in love and married a fine Christian woman, no longer pining away after Jane.

8. *You have repeatedly endangered your health and shortened your life.*

Self-sacrifice is required when we set ourselves to live lovingly. But remember that all self-sacrifice is not love, according to Scripture. Examine your self-sacrificing, especially if it's a habit. Or if it becomes a denial of your value.

KEEP YOUR BALANCE

It's possible to become mired in self-analysis, to become so fixated on our own inner workings that we lose touch with the rest of the world. Too much introspection can be harmful, just as too little can make us strangers to ourselves.

If you do take a thoughtful look at your history, be careful to keep your balance. Don't become totally self-absorbed in your attempt to analyze what went wrong. It's probably healthier to do this kind of mental work a little at a time, keeping the rest of your life intact. Try to maintain a reasonable balance of work, play, rest, humor, and satisfying relationships with your family and friends.

A balanced life in her day-to-day routine is especially necessary to a woman trying to think through the events of her past. Focus too intensely on the past, and you'll lose the ability to see it clearly. You will also run the risk of becoming so involved in yourself that you cannot give any love away.

Some problems are severe enough to require outside help. If you sense that's the case, do whatever is needed to receive that outside help. Ask your pastor to help you find the kind of medical or specialized therapy suitable for your needs.

LOVE COUNTERFEITS

In following chapters, we'll discuss specific counterfeit loves, how they hinder our relationships, and how we can grow out of them to a more healthy way of loving. We'll take a look at the Rescuer who enables an abuser while calling it "Christian love."

Then, chapter 4 addresses the confusion many victimized women feel regarding their Christian duty to forgive, to bear all things, and to love unconditionally. This woman can find relief without violating her beliefs about her duty to God. As she recognizes patterns that set her up to be a Victim time and again, she can change unhealthy ways of relating.

The Matriarch typifies the woman who confuses love with absolute control. Legitimate parental control turns into a need to shape and mold her child in the ways she knows are "best for her." With amazing determination and force of will, she "loves" the people in her family.

The Romantic is hung up on romance, in love with the idea of being in love. She's as hooked on the powerful emotions of "falling in love" as any junkie is hooked on his heroin. Falling in love brings her such heady excitement that other satisfactions and joys seem bland in comparison. Her problems with love do not revolve around the pain she's felt but around the pleasure.

The Angel is a busy person, doing what everyone else wants done, "denying" herself day after day and wondering why she's feeling angry with God. This capable, conscientious, godly woman has heard too many sermons defining love as service, sacrifice, and self-denial. She needs to examine the scriptures that allow her to love herself!

The Addict is someone who confuses sex with love. She feels loved only when it is expressed sexually, or when she knows she is the object of sexual desire.

Possibly the most dangerous counterfeit, Obsession, is a subject rarely addressed in Sunday sermons. Yet many obsessed persons sit through Sunday sermons on love. They come away with copious notes, filled with hope and added substance to their obsession. Robin's experience, recounted in the introduction, was one that touched close to me.

Being lovable is basic to life for the Darling. She was such a cute little girl. Always cuddled, held, and told she was lovable, she forgot to grow beyond the childish delight of being the Darling.

CATEGORIES—ARE THEY EVER REAL?

While categories are a convenient way of organizing ideas, they are not meant to be applied rigidly. If I had to tag myself with one of the counterfeit love labels, such as Romantic or Matriarch, I would have difficulty choosing one. At some time or another, I have identified, at least to a degree, with each of them. That is because these thinking errors are common ones. You may, for example, believe yourself far removed from the woman described as the Addict, yet you recognize some of her tendencies as quite familiar.

You are a unique, one-of-a-kind creation of God, and it is impossible to invent one category to accurately describe you. Any label would be too narrow, too limited in scope to represent all of you. Even when I label myself a Rescuer in chapter 3, I am referring to tendencies I have noticed. I am describing not who I really am; this is not the *real* me, underneath it all.

These categories are descriptions of certain patterns of behavior, many of which each of us falls into at times. The important thing is not to figure out where you fit, but to recognize beliefs and misconceptions that need to be changed, and to move beyond any of these patterns of behavior that have become invisible traps.

A CATEGORY IS NOT YOUR IDENTITY

Neither are these labels intended as a handy guide for

categorizing others, like some sort of zodiac chart. I resent anyone telling me all about myself on the basis of the month I was born, and do not believe it is fair to prejudge others because of one experience or poor choice in the area of love. Your mistakes are not your identity. Nor are your behavior patterns or your illusions about love.

Disappointment in love often brings confusion about our true identity. For a Christian woman, identity is found not in love, but in a relationship with God. That secure identity does not change when you fail in a love relationship or experience rejection. When you understand that, you will cease searching for identity in a person to love. You will return your focus to the source of your identity, Jesus Christ. Loving another person will never show you who you really are. In fact, using another person to gain a sense of identity will only work against love. (Are you loving him or using him?)

Ask Jesus to repair the chips and cracks, show you again who you are, and move on to live out that actual, true identity.

Love at its best flows from the woman who has been made whole by Jesus. She has established a strong awareness of her identity. Her love expresses the essence of her person to everyone around her, whether her children, church friends, neighbors, or sweetheart.

The biggest mistake we can make in handling past failures is to give up on love. The risks of loving are great. They are many. Loving is not safe! But the risks of *not* loving are greater and far more damaging. A person who chooses not to love can conceivably live a safe, sterile life. But is it really life at all?

3
...

The Rescuer

"Listen to your heart."

"Trust your feelings."

"Should I marry Jim?" "Well, what is your heart telling you? Are you in love with him?"

In matters of romance and marriage, most of us grow up believing a collection of mismatched clichés that appear in popular songs, TV love stories, and magazine ads. The heart is the final authority in our society. A woman who goes against her feelings in a romantic choice is quickly labeled as making a big mistake. It's practically a crime in a woman's view of herself to *not* marry a man with whom she falls in love. Even if the man is a proven criminal or a dangerous psychopath!

In fact, a subtle undercurrent in our folk theology suggests it's noble and glamorous to fall in love with a bad

guy. We could quote popular songs about that idea, too.
They became popular for a good reason. Thousands of
people identify with the sentiments these songs express.

A song from a former era is entitled, "It Had to be You."
The singer croons,

Some others I've seen might never be mean,
Might never be cross or try to be boss,
But they wouldn't do.
Nobody else gave me a thrill;
With all your faults I love you still.
It had to be you, wonderful you; it had to be you.

Sounds like the best reason to get married, right? After
all, if he gave me a thrill, what more proof do I need?
Obviously, it's real love, the genuine article.

WILD BOYS

Sometimes nice girls from good Christian homes fall in
love with wild boys. It's likely to be quite exciting, not
only because she's fascinated by someone so different
from herself, but also because an immature rebel's irresponsible behavior keeps things stirred up. His volatile or
aggressive personality may assume the aura of macho,
masculine attractiveness. His impulsiveness and unpre-
dictability keep the people around him on the edge of
excitement.

A young girl in love with this macho man will find her
emotions intensified because of the roller coaster ride he
gives her with his ups and downs of kindness and cruelty,
weakness and strength, sweetness and sarcasm. But the
thrills are deceptive. Living with a man like this is neither
romantic nor thrilling after long. Too soon, she awakens
from her romantic daydream to realize she is imprisoned in

a real-life nightmare. The emotions she thought were love have disappeared. Instead, her emotions have turned to fear, confusion, or self-hatred.

THE NEED TO BE NEEDED

Some rescuers act not out of love, but out of an unconscious fear that they will only be loved if they are needed. In her book, *Women Who Love Too Much*, Robin Norwood shares the stories of many women caught in destructive romances through this need to be needed. Pam, for example, put it this way:

I could never have put it into words when I was growing up, but the only way I knew how to be with someone, especially someone male, was if he needed me. Then he wouldn't leave me, because I'd be helping him and he'd be grateful.

Not surprisingly, my first boyfriend was crippled. Now, he was a nice enough boy, and certainly a girl could have enjoyed being with him just for his company. But I had another reason. I was with him because it was *safe*; since I was doing him a favor, I wouldn't be rejected and get hurt. . . . I was really crazy about this boy, but I know now that I chose him because, like me, he had something wrong with *him*. His flaw showed, so I could be comfortable feeling all this pain and pity for him. He was, by far, my healthiest boyfriend. After him came juvenile delinquents, underachievers—losers, all of them.

When I was 17 I met my first husband. He was in trouble in school and flunking out. His father and mother were divorced but still fighting with each other. Compared to his background, mine looked good! I could relax a little and not feel so ashamed.

And of course, I felt so sorry for him. He was quite a rebel, but I thought that was because no one before me had ever really understood him.[1]

NOT ALL BAD LUCK

This was only Pam's first in a series of rescuing relationships. Looking back later, she said,

It still wasn't clear to me ... that I had a pattern of picking men who were not, in my opinion, fine just as they were, but rather whom I saw as needing my help. I only caught on to that after several more relationships with impossible men: one was addicted to pot; one was gay; one was impotent; and ... one supposedly unhappily married. When that involvement ended (disastrously), I couldn't continue to believe it was all bad luck. I know I must have had a part in what had happened to me.[2]

Pam's story, all too common, was a life full of sadness and pain. Like her, women repeat the pattern over and over, never quite getting it right. They don't suspect that their "love" is actually a self-destructive habit of rescuing in hopes of receiving love. The feelings have fooled them; they've bought a counterfeit.

KIND-HEARTED CHRISTIANS

Romantic relationships are only one place where a rescuer becomes confused. Among Christians who actively minister to others, who is so wise to have never found herself confused or feeling "in over her head"?

It is good and right to want to help others. To deeply care to the point of disregarding consequences to oneself can be a mark of spiritual maturity. Many compassionate people choose careers in nursing, teaching, or social work so that they can help others. Mental health, counseling, psychology, and pastoral ministry are other "helping professions."

In these careers, as in many others, the talent most necessary is also the quality that can create the most problems. When you feel empathy with a hurting person, he or she is often healed through the simple presence of your caring compassion. Jesus displayed this quality and left his followers with the ability to live compassionate lives. But Rescuers don't stop at merely feeling. Motivated by inside forces of love, we enter into the needs as if they were our own pain. Sometimes we lose our own sense of separateness.

EVEN PROFESSIONAL RESCUERS CAN FAIL

Famous psychologist Carl Rogers tells about his own experience with this. Looking back on both the joys and discouragements of his long career, he described an instance where a

serious crisis built around an incredibly lengthy, poorly handled therapeutic relationship which I had with a severely schizophrenic girl. The story is a long one, but suffice it to say that partly because I was so determined to help her, I got to the point where I could not separate my "self" from hers. I literally lost my "self," lost the boundaries of myself. The efforts of colleagues to help me were of no avail, and I became convinced (and I think with some reason) that I was going insane.[3]

This man, known around the world for his study of

empathy, who proved conclusively the power of empathic listening, was not afraid to admit to his own difficulties with it. Highly trained and experienced as he was, he was still vulnerable in this area.

I have experienced difficulty in this area and learned many painful lessons through it. Because I was a Christian, intent on loving as Christ loves, with boundless compassion, concern, acceptance, and forgiveness, I interpreted my feelings as quite positive. I assumed I must be growing spiritually because of my ability to respond so intensely and lovingly to someone else's needs.

APPROPRIATE RESCUING

When we Rescuers find ourselves in this state of inordinate concern, we lose our objectivity and become part of the problem. Now we need someone to rescue us. Fortunately for Carl Rogers, his wife knew when to practice *appropriate rescuing*:

One morning after an hour or so at the office I simply panicked. I walked home and told Helen, "I've got to get out of here. Far away!" She, of course, knew something of what I had been going through, but her reply was balm to my soul. She said, "Okay, let's go right now." After a few phone calls to staff members to ask them to take over my responsibilities, and some hasty packing, we were on the road inside of two hours and didn't return for more than six weeks. I had my ups and downs, and when I returned I went into therapy with one of my colleagues, gaining great help ... during this whole period Helen was certain this state of mind would pass away, that I was not insane, and showed in every way how much she cared.[4]

There is, then, a time when rescuing is an appropriate way to love. Especially when a Christian has fallen into the quicksand of his own compassion. Like Dr. Rogers' wife, my partner exercised wisdom, stepped in, and saved me from my delusions of grandeur. Without criticizing, blaming, or lecturing, Jerry carried me off to a restful retreat and simply let me regain my balance in an environment of love and understanding. Jerry's loyalty and commitment to me at a time of such personal disappointment was doubtless the best therapy a misguided Rescuer could receive.

Too often, those in the helping professions are tied to an image of perfection and are not allowed to fall. If they trip up in just one out of hundreds of helping relationships, they risk loss of public confidence and sometimes outright punishment. "A hypocrite!" we say, "a phony all along."

NEEDED: ROOM TO GROW

As Christians, we sometimes more easily forgive those who steal, murder, or deal drugs than we do those who sin in their attempt to love. We expect a lot of each other, especially of those in positions of visible leadership. But if they are to grow in love, we must allow for an occasional fumble. Great growth can come from failure if it is not used as an excuse to stop loving.

This kind of experience is nothing new, of course. We have reason to believe Christians of the first century church met with it in their enthusiasm for the Gospel. Paul wrote to the Galatians, "If someone is caught in a sin, you who are spiritual should restore him gently. *But watch yourself*, or you also may be tempted" (Gal. 6:10, italics added). He continues with some warnings about overestimating our importance and forgetting our human vulnerability.

At the same time, Paul didn't want Rescuers to quit

helping people. "Let us not become weary in doing good, for at the proper time we will reap a harvest if we do not give up. Therefore, as we have opportunity, let us do good to all people, especially to those who belong to the family of believers" (Gal. 6:9, 10).

PRESCRIPTION FOR THE CHRISTIAN HELPER

At first glance, we may overlook the common sense and practical wisdom for Rescuers contained in this section of scripture. However, it is the perfect prescription for us, especially since it appears in the middle of two chapters on love. In fact, it immediately follows the verse about the fruit of the Spirit, each of which is simply a manifestation of love.

Paul contrasts these ways of relating with an ugly list he calls the "works of the flesh" or "acts of the sinful nature." One list depicts people hating each other, fighting, competing, envying, exploiting, and hurting. Another list describes people who treat each other with respect and value. They show patience toward one another, make peace rather than cause contention, control themselves, and behave kindly. These people are loyal and trustworthy. They are tolerant of one another's imperfections and failures. They are generous, good, and kind. When the Galatian believers first read these lists, they must have responded, "Of course this is the way we want to be! Who would want to hang around with that first group anyway?"

But as they committed themselves to loving relationships, Paul knew, they would wonder sometimes whether it was worth it. Especially after a big fumble that won few cheers from the stands.

In the aftermath of a bungled relationship, you experience feelings of self-recrimination. But because you were honestly trying to help someone in need, these feelings may be even stronger as you see things more clearly and realize your over-involved emotions victimized both you and the other person. It's quite natural to have thoughts such as:

How could I be so stupid?
Why did I waste so much time on such a hopeless case?
Look at all the things I've neglected while being so absorbed in her problems.

LEARNING FROM DISILLUSIONMENT

Later, disillusionment enters:
Why did God let me think I was loving?
So this is where it gets you if you let yourself care!

Although you might not verbalize it, you feel resentment: *All that time, all that work, and what is there to show for it? She's no better for all my helping!*

A frustrated pastor said, "It's hard to watch people mess up their lives. I've spent hours counseling with Joe and Mary, praying with them, going over scriptures. Still their marriage is no better. He's even talking divorce. I find myself laying awake nights worrying about them. I pray for them, but they don't change. I'm even angry with them because my prayers aren't being answered."

We like to see results. We are product-oriented. We even put ourselves on a spiritual productivity schedule where the results must be visible, measurable, and above all, speedy.

God sees it from the vantage of eternity. Yet he knows how we think, and to encourage us, he graciously uses the illustration of sowing and reaping. "I am taking note," he says, "and whether or not any of your fellow humans see or understand your gifts of love, I will make sure they are laid up for you in your eternal investment account."

The disillusionment stage is highly valuable because if

we allow ourselves to ask those frightening questions and listen to God's answers, we'll learn truths that we'll never forget. These truths will bring a gradual but permanent change to our ways of "helping." We may continue to be Rescuers, but with a well-defined sense of when our rescuing is or is not an act of genuine love.

RESCUING AS AUTHENTIC LOVE

For the past five years, I have joined with many other parents in a rescue operation to establish early intervention for school children who show signs of drug abuse. In our school district, parents and school personnel do not want to stand helplessly watching as children become addicted. Knowing the suffering ahead for them, we have begun to invest our time and money in prevention.

Along with educating parents, children, teachers, and school counselors about drug and alcohol abuse, we have set up procedures that we use to spot children who have begun using. We then provide them and their parents the opportunity to get help. This is an example of appropriate rescuing.

MESSIAH COMPLEX

As anyone who works in the treatment field can attest, one person working alone to "cure" an addict will almost certainly fail, or at the very least, wear herself out with frustration. We start out with exaggerated notions of our ability to "save" a person in this condition, only to be sadly disappointed. We believe "love will conquer all." If only I love enough, encourage enough, help her feel worthwhile, believe God will heal her.

A woman who falls in love with an alcoholic often feels she can love him out of the disease. Without realizing it, she may develop a Messiah complex, feeling herself responsible to single-handedly rescue him. The care and concern she feels for him are genuine love. But when she crosses the line into a Messiah complex, she begins to do things that are actually the opposite of love.

She takes responsibility on herself that is rightfully her husband's alone. In her attempt to save him from the results of his addiction, she cushions him from consequences he ought to experience. He doesn't feel the effects of his habit. Her rescuing becomes enabling.

Enabling is a term often heard today in discussions on alcoholism and addiction. The enabler is the person who makes it possible for the addict to continue his habit. Not always because she supplies the drugs or the money, but because she always forgives his violence, picks up the pieces, covers for him, or simply holds him and assures him everything will be all right. He keeps denying that he has a problem and with well-meaning intentions, she helps him believe the rationalizations he uses to avoid getting help.

A TIME TO STOP

If you are this woman, love demands you stop rescuing. Short-term rescuing, that is. Let him feel the full impact of his habit. Join with others to plan a strategy of intervention that will face him squarely with the effects of his behavior on those he loves. Call a halt to his denial, his pretending, and your buying into his lies and excuses.

You need the help and support of others. It is not only sensible, but godly to admit you can't do it alone, not even with God's help. God wants to get some other people involved in this rescue operation; perhaps your parents, his parents, brothers, sisters, and possibly professionals. By acknowledging your need for help from others, you'll be giving up your Messiah complex.

While you're doing all this, you won't feel like the kind, sweet, forgiving Rescuer anymore. The firm actions you initiate may feel uncomfortable, even frightening. "This just isn't me! I don't think I can do this," said Pam, who had finally stopped enabling her husband after fifteen years.

Love is acting for the highest good of another. It is caring as much about the well-being of another as about your own well-being. The Bible give us no guarantee that love will always *feel* comfortable, nor that love is something you feel at all. Love is what you do. Continuing with the status quo may feel like the most comfortable thing to do, but when that includes closing your eyes or refusing to take action while a deadly disease destroys a loved one, *it is not love.*

Bright red stop lights do not immediately flash when it is time to stop rescuing and begin loving in another fashion. Because we must never give up our compassion, we will always risk error. No pat answers exist other than "Don't get involved." Obviously not an answer! You *will* get involved, risk or no risk.

BIBLICAL TRUTHS FOR RESCUERS

As you take that risk, you may find that this list of biblical truths will help you know when your rescuing is or is not an act of genuine love. If you suspect your emotions are misleading you, use this list to examine yourself and your subjective beliefs:

1. *"Results" in another person's life are not my responsibility.*

2. *My preconceived notions of what the "product" of my helping should be may be light years away from God's actual intentions.*

3. *I cannot change another person, no matter how much*

I care and want to help.

4. *No strings are attached to my gift of love.* My love is not real if it comes with conditions, for example, "I listened when you were hurting. I showed you some scriptures and told you what you ought to do. Now you owe it to me to follow my advice."

5. *I am not needed in the role of Messiah.* God is at work in the other person. He is the Messiah.

6. *I must never overestimate my ability to know what is best for another.*

7. *I must never underestimate my human vulnerability.* It is possible to jump into the water and sink with the drowning victim.

8. *I am not superior. I am just a friend, a person who has chosen to love.* Love is never proud, arrogant, or impressed with itself. If putting myself in the position of "helper" brings feelings of superiority, I must recognize that those motivations are not love. I choose to love people because God loves them and because they are valuable, not because I see it as a chance to feel superior, even if benevolently so.

9. *Only eternity will reveal the fruit of love I have sown in others' lives.* Therefore I can relax as I give to those in need, trusting God to use my gifts as he pleases.

10. *When I love another person, I offer it as a gift to Christ.* The recipient of my gift may or may not respond in the way I expect. But her response neither invalidates nor affirms my choice to love. The response that really matters is God's words, "Well done, thou good and faithful servant."

The above simple truth is one of the most freeing, comforting, and encouraging things the Lord ever taught me about ministry. I learned it in my driveway, just as I stepped wearily out of the car at the end of a highly disappointing day.

49

That morning I received a call in my office that appeared to be an answer to our prayers for a young woman I'd tried hard to help overcome certain handicaps. I immediately contacted Jenny with the good news. If she would respond to the opportunity that day, a bright future and career could open up to her.

"Yes, I'll help," I said, realizing that I would have to reschedule the day's appointments. "Thank you, Lord, for dropping this open door into Jenny's lap today." Giving up the day's work seemed a small price compared to what this might mean for Jenny.

A DECISION OF FEAR

It turned out to be a long day, too, because Jenny could not walk through that door into the life she'd said she wanted. She went with me, handled herself well, and then lost her nerve. I tried to hide my shock as we drank several cups of coffee and talked it over. Perhaps she needed more encouragement. We could go back. . . .

She never did go back. At the end of the afternoon, I knew she would not. She allowed fear to control her, and I couldn't do a thing about it. "God, I was sure this opportunity was from you. I gave up a whole day thinking I was obeying you. Why did it turn out like this?!"

Silence. No answer. "Guess I wasted my day. I don't even know where I went wrong." I arrived home, stepped out onto the driveway, and closed the car door behind me.

"Who are you working for, Barbara? Does Jenny call the shots? Does she decide whether you did the right thing? Is her response the proof that you're doing my will?"

"Of course not; that girl hasn't the common sense to run her own life!"

"You did what I asked you to do today. It's not your job to determine what will come out of it. 'Some plant, others water, it is God who gives the increase.' Remember?"

I walked into the house with these words occupying my mind and reached for a Bible.

"For Christ's love compels us, because we are convinced that one died for all, and therefore all died. And he died for all, that those who live should no longer *live for themselves but for him* who died for them and was raised again" (2 Cor. 5:14-15 italics added).

This is the ultimate good news for the Rescuer! The love inside that prompts me to reach out to the hurting person is from God. My motivation is from him. The love of Christ is a compelling love; it moves me to action. But I must offer the action back to him. It is Christ I am living for; not results, not responses from those I attempt to help, not success, not change, not pride in my accomplishments, not even the good feelings I get from helping.

ONLY AN ASSISTANT

As the Savior's servant, I am delivered from the need to be a savior. At best, I am only an assistant. He has a bit more experience in this delicate business. I'll let him give the directions and take responsibility for the outcome.

As a servant of Christ, I have a guaranteed wage. My salary (eternal reward) is permanent. I don't need to see a daily paycheck as proof I actually did the work I was to do. Most of the time the rewards of loving are rich in themselves; if not, I am assured that in God's kingdom there is no such thing as wasted love. My part is to live a life of love by taking the risks and learning from my mistakes. His part is to separate the wheat from the chaff, keeping the part of my love that is genuine. It is one of the few things I will take with me into the next world.

4
...
The Victim

Patricia Hearst, beloved daughter of the wealthy Hearst family, was heiress to one of the world's famous fortunes. At nineteen, she became the victim of a bizarre, outrageous kidnapping. Strange men and women burst into her apartment, overpowered her boyfriend, and carried her kicking and screaming into their car. Her story made headlines for every newspaper in the country. We listened, horrified, to her traumatized fiance's story on the evening news.

Not long afterward, she was again the top story. Not because the police had found and rescued her, as we were praying would happen. But because, brandishing a machine gun and yelling something about expropriating capitalist funds for the poor, she and her captors had robbed a bank.

The bank's cameras had captured the sensational robbery in living color for all the world to see. This was exactly what her captors wanted in their deranged, destructive quest for power. Now our victim Patty had a new problem. Along with her kidnappers, the Symbionese Liberation Army, she was a fugitive, wanted on robbery charges. Actually they were no army at all, merely a small group of weird radicals.

At first, we believed the SLA had forced her to commit these crimes. Then the media and her family received taped messages from Patty herself. The next sensational story: Patricia Hearst appeared to have fallen in love with Cujo, one of her tormentors. She had joined his war against the wealthy and powerful, including her own family.

Later we discovered the terrorists had used old and proven brainwashing techniques. When a human being is made to feel totally humiliated, fearful, deprived, and helpless in the hands of a cruel persecutor, that person becomes extremely vulnerable. She is responsive to the slightest show of kindness from that same cruel persecutor. The illusion of power he represents in the face of desperate powerlessness causes an exaggerated emotional response in his victim.

In the dark abyss of misery where all feelings are only painful fear or despair, one solitary pleasant emotion is like a drop of water on the tongue of a perishing desert traveler. The deliciousness of that emotion, be it hope, or the feeling, "He cares—someone cares for me!" is a hook. The victim wants to feel it again. Based on their knowledge of these dynamics, experts speculated about Patty's "love."

Years later, after Patty recovered from the terrifying ordeal, she told her own story in a book,[1] a movie, and public interviews. She was a victim all right, but not of love, of fear. She had never been "in love" with her captors; they were repugnant and disgusting to her. They had locked her in a dark closet for fifty-seven days and terrorized her until she believed they held absolute power. They seemed invincible, totally heartless, and definitely insane! She had no hope of escape and no options; she felt she had to do whatever they commanded or die.

Fighting was useless; she would suffer less if she submitted passively to their demands, be they sex, bank robbery, or reading scripted statements into a tape recorder. She let them preach their bizarre doctrine to her for hours on end, then parroted it back to them. *What choice do I have?* she thought. So, when the chance for freedom came, she was so brainwashed she believed her rescuers were out to kill her. Gradually, she had become the victim, no longer of the SLA, but of her own fear and hopelessness. The SLA convinced her that her parents, the police, or the FBI would shoot her on sight.

Consequently, it was two years before she saw her family again, even though all but two of the terrorists were dead, and she could have escaped.

Through no fault of her own, Patty Hearst became a victim; physically, mentally, and emotionally. The suffering she endured and the process by which she ended up a prisoner of her own fears and beliefs is much the same as the experiences of other victimized women. Women who have not been kidnapped by radicals, but who have been terrorized by abusive boyfriends, fathers, or husbands.

Some of them would recognize the thoughts and feelings Patty describes in her book. The hopelessness, fear, and the powerlessness are all too familiar. Someone who offers help is not necessarily warmly received as a rescuer. Some of these women actually do consider themselves "in love" with their tormentors and don't appreciate interference. At first glance, this is hard to understand.

It's a puzzling question: why do women love men who mistreat them? (Or for that matter, why do men love women who mistreat them?) A rather naive explanation was once widely accepted by psychologists and pastors. They believed these women were masochists, that is, persons who experience pleasure in pain.

They bring pain upon themselves, either deliberately or subconsciously. Not a very compassionate explanation! Nowadays, it is solidly disproven as a cause-effect theory by which we can lump all victimized women into a neat, tidy category.

HIGH INTENSITY EMOTIONS

Many women who love abusive men are confused by emotional counterfeits of love. For example, many prostitutes "love" their pimp. The pimp maintains his control by a calculated interchange of rejection and affection, beating and loving, and insults that tear at her self-worth unexpectedly followed by hope of winning his approval.

When our emotions are raised to high intensity, as they are in times of attack on our person, we are especially vulnerable to someone who wants power over us. In those times of extremity, even the most stable woman is at risk of mis-labeling what she feels. While it may be accurate to say, "This feels pleasant," it may be far from the truth to conclude, "This is love."

A pretty girl in our high school broke up with her steady boyfriend. "Wonder why? He's so cute and such a football star!" was the talk in the girls' locker room.

"I know why," said Cindy. "He beat her up—twice. She came to school with a black eye one Monday a few weeks ago, after a weekend date with that cutie!"

To my young, romantic mind, it seemed incomprehensible that a guy would take a girl out, spend money on gas, hamburgers, and fries, and then end the evening punching her out. That didn't make sense! What made even less sense was that she went out with him again after that. Then, after graduation, this girl married her abuser!

CAUSES

One side of the issue has to do with causes. Why do men become abusive in the first place? For some, it was modeled in their parents' relationship. Others were abused children. Some even believe it's macho to kick their women around: "You gotta let her know who's boss!"

Some men simply never learned self-control. Others are neurotically angry. Many men hate women while appearing to love them. Whatever the background factors, be assured women are *not* the cause (unless they tolerate or excuse the abuse). You may be told it's your fault he lost control, for example, if you just wouldn't burn the potatoes. . . . These accusations are not true. If anyone is mistreating you, emotionally or physically, there is *no* excuse. You have the right to be treated with respect. No man, woman, or child has any valid reason to violate that right.

SUFFERING IN SILENCE

During a recent trip to the supermarket, I noticed a couple loading their groceries into the car. Actually, *she* was loading the car while keeping the baby balanced in the cart. Husband was watching impatiently. As he finished his ice cream bar, he shouted rudely, "Come on, Mom! Hurry up! Let's go!"

I wondered how "Mom" felt. Did she ever stop to question the way he spoke to her? Did it occur to her that he probably didn't bark orders like that to his friends? Or if he did, that his friends hadn't stuck around? Does she silently endure, quoting to herself scriptures about patience and longsuffering? Does she believe she is *loving* him by showing such silent subservience? Young "Mom" was allowing verbal abuse, and I suspect it was worse in private.

Why does any woman allow herself to be mistreated? How does she rationalize acceptance of such treatment? Why does she not insist that she be treated with respect?

Some of us are just chicken. We'd rather blame someone else for our unhappiness than stand up for ourselves and bring on what may turn into conflict.

We're good at smoothing things over. We try to avoid unpleasant discussions and intimidating scenes. We live by those old clichés, "Let sleeping dogs lie," and "Don't rock the boat." Some of us even Christianize our cowardice. We call it submission. Or turning the other cheek. Or, worst of all, unconditional love!

Sometimes Christian women hold a false image of femininity and equate it with passivity. We are purposely non-assertive, believing that God created women as responders and men as initiators. If we have this all tangled up with our image of God, we're locked neatly into a mental trap similar to the one that kept Patty Hearst from freedom.

If we believe passivity is spiritual, we not only feel guilty whenever we assert ourselves or speak up when mistreated, we also believe God is unhappy with us. We have failed him. We have failed to be *the* Christian woman who at all times ignores insults, forgives abuse and bodily harm, and sweetly prays for her sinful abuser.

HOW TO DESTROY INTIMACY

Victims who live out this belief system in their close relationships suffer serious damage to their self-respect. Repressed anger and resentment along with a growing loss of intimacy is part of the package.

Emotional intimacy can only develop between two real people who share an open and honest relationship. They must let each other know what they feel and think. They must, if they value their relationship, tell each other when something hurts. They must speak up if they feel mistreated, ignored, neglected, rejected, or confused.

When a woman keeps her hurts and wounded pride to herself, silently forgiving either a careless husband or loud-mouthed teenager, she is not helping anyone. No matter how sincerely she believes she is doing the will of God, she is *not* doing the will of God! She is creating a monster. Perhaps several monsters.

Question: How do you grow a monster?

Answer: Just keep feeding the baby dragon.

If I don't deal with selfish or disrespectful behavior, the abusers will assume that behavior is acceptable. They will continue it, possibly unaware that it is hurtful to me. Love demands I confront any attempts to control me by intimidation, coercion, threats, yelling, or insults.

GENUINE CARING

If I genuinely love the person who is acting abusively, I will, at the very least, give him the opportunity to know my thoughts and feelings. I want him to know how his actions affect others so he can change them rather than risk destroying all of his close relationships.

This is not punishment. It is caring communication. Rather than retaliate with hurtful actions, I choose to forgive. But forgiveness is not all there is to love. The silent, passive doormat can pride herself on remarkable feats of forgiveness, while the baby dragon grows strong on his rich diet. What disillusionment she faces when one day she discovers a full-grown, fire-breathing monster.

By referring to the dragon as male, I do not wish to imply, and certainly do not believe, that men are always the culprits in abuse. Statistically, more men than women are found guilty of *physical* abuse. But husband abuse is not uncommon. There are violent women too. I suspect that if someone gathered statistics on *emotional* abuse, at least as many women as men would be implicated.

Women are capable of using abusive tactics to control others, and they disguise those tactics in feminine wiles and manipulative games.

TRUST IS NOT ALWAYS LOVE

Chronic victims often have distorted thinking about trust. Those who are upright, kind, and good assume other people are upright, kind, and good. The charge, "You don't trust me!" comes at this woman like a fiery arrow. She is hurt, insulted, and ashamed. She feels guilty, as though she has committed some great sin in failing to trust. Any failure to trust people, especially people close to her, seems to her a moral failure. God wants her to trust, doesn't he?

A mother notices subtle changes in her teenager, the kind of changes that signal drug use. Worried, she searches his room and comes across evidence that confirms her fears. What does the teenager say when she confronts him? "You had no right to search my room! That's an invasion of privacy!"

Mother feels like she's the guilty one; her attention turns to defending herself, and the angry teen stalks out the door.

Experts claim that parents' ambivalence toward trust is a key reason kids can get so deeply hooked on drugs before their parents find out. Statistics show that the average teen drug abuser has used drugs for at least two years before his parents discover anything.

To communicate this statistic, our PTA made a poster for parents. We drew a large ostrich with its head in the sand. The ostrich appears at school events where we ask parents to sign the "parent pledge" against teen drug and alcohol use. The sign says, "Don't be an ostrich." The ostrich symbolizes the human tendency we all recognize: if we can't see the danger, maybe it isn't there. Or stated differently, "Ignore it and it will go away."

"Where *are* these parents?" asked one mother in our local PTA. "How could they not know?"

As we speculated, one said, "They must be in denial, just refusing to face the truth."

"Yes, but on the other hand," inserted another mother, "don't we all try to trust our kids? Don't we try to believe the best? I've always thought that's what we're supposed to do."

Yes, the Bible says "[Love] always protects, always trusts, always hopes, always perseveres" (1 Cor. 13:7). But the very same passage also says love "does not delight in evil but rejoices with the truth" (1 Cor. 13:6).

LOVE AND TRUTH

Love is not afraid of truth. Love does not indulge evil but seeks to know the truth so the destructive effects of evil can be addressed. Love has the courage to face evil squarely.

Genuine love seeks the highest good of the loved one and has the audacity to believe it can happen. It will persevere because it maintains hope and sees the best still present in that hurting loved one. It loves him at his worst because it sees a brighter day ahead.

Love also *protects*. When it comes to protecting our children from dangers such as drug and alcohol use, we must balance trust with wisdom. Guarding our children's safety and their future is an important part of love.

When we see trust in its proper context, we understand that the trust of the Bible is not blind trust. It is not closing our eyes to impending tragedy and repeating over and over, "I must trust. I must trust."

Biblical love does not ignore reality. It doesn't run from

the truth while mouthing soft words about love and trust.

THE DANGERS OF MISPLACED TRUST

In Seattle, it was quite a media event when convicted serial murderer Ted Bundy was executed in the electric chair. Local TV channels interrupted their regular programming with hour-long specials, interviews with victims' parents, psychologists, detectives, writers, former Bundy defenders, and advocates for and against the death penalty.

Bundy's killing began with women from our own university. Some investigators believe he murdered more than one hundred women. Police detectives in at least five states, sometimes full-time task forces, worked incessantly to identify and catch this psychopath, yet his killing continued for four years before he was arrested in Florida.

Ted Bundy almost never hid; he appeared normal to everyone who knew him. Even his long-time lover Liz couldn't believe he was the "Ted murderer." In retrospect, it seems preposterous that he walked our streets in broad daylight, unafraid for years. At night, he captured, raped, and killed pretty college girls, usually carefully chosen: they were all smart, had nice figures, and wore long hair parted in the middle. For awhile, he killed one every month, sometimes two at a time. How did he get away with it for so long?

Women trusted Ted. Charming, intelligent, and well-groomed, Ted didn't look like a sex criminal. Although a psychopath, a man without a conscience, he had constructed a carefully devised facade designed to win a woman's trust and win it quickly.

Sometimes he added credence to the facade by appearing to be injured. He wore a fake cast on his arm or leg and asked girls to help him pick up the books he'd just dropped.

Or he posed as a policeman or fireman; who would question the intentions of these authority figures? Some of his victims were even the daughters of police or fire officials; they were not naive girls. Yet they fell for this ploy.

Ted Bundy used women when he wasn't murdering. Even after he was sent to prison, he collected a following of "Ted groupies," as they were known. Ann Rule, author of a book on Ted Bundy, noted:

> I looked around the courtroom. . . . The front row—just behind Ted and the defense team—was jammed with pretty young women, as it would be each day. Did they *know* how much they resembled the . . . victims? Their eyes never left Ted, and they blushed and giggled with delight when he turned to flash a blinding smile at them, as he often did. Outside the courtroom, some of them would admit to reporters that Ted frightened them, yet they couldn't stay away. It is a common syndrome, this fascination that an alleged mass killer has for some women, as if he was the ultimate macho figure.[2]

The tragedy of the Ted murders lies in the feminine ability to trust. A misplaced trust; a trust that should have been examined. How many lives could have been saved, how many parents spared loss if only. . . .

If only what? If only one woman had believed her doubts and called the police when she saw the newspaper pictures. When two of them finally did call, it was too late for the Washington victims. Ann Rule writes touchingly of her own feelings and also observes,

> Ted's retinue of friends . . . was always heavily weighted with women. Some loved him as a man.

Some women, like myself, were drawn to his courtly manners, his little boy quality, his seemingly genuine concern and thoughtfulness. ... Because he could control women, balance us carefully in the tightly structured world he had manufactured, we were important to him. He dangled us as puppets from a string, and when one of us did not react as he wanted, he was both outraged and confused.[3]

The women in Ted's life were so concerned with their own emotions and relationships with him that they couldn't take action. Their minds set aside the nagging but critical question, *Could he be the Ted killer?* to ponder instead, *What does he think of me ... What if I upset him? How could I stand to lose him?* This was true not only of those romantically involved, but also of the older women to whom he had endeared himself. They obscured the truth behind a fog of heady emotions.

MARRIED TO A MANIAC

Lindsay sat in my office one day describing a terrifying marriage to a man who, judging from his insane behavior, was clearly a maniac. I marvelled that she had survived the stress for four years.

This man's psychosis took on a religious flavor. When it took him over, he shouted murderous threats in the language of an Old Testament prophet. This delusion is evidence of a complete psychotic break with reality and the kind of thing that often precedes violence done "because God told me to." Nothing to fool around with!

Lindsay was a new Christian when she married Bart; he taught her the Bible, and especially that he, the husband, was her spiritual leader, and she must obey him. When he quoted scripture, or what sounded like scripture, she was completely intimidated. After all, he was the expert in the deeper things of God, she the ignorant, unlearned one. Only recently had she shaken herself awake and asked the question, "Could this man have a mental problem?" By then she had borne a child whose safety was clearly in question.

Bart's insanity became apparent to some neighbors one day and later at his work. He began disappearing for days at a time with no explanation. Eventually he was arrested for burglary, and in time, the process of court trials and examinations revealed the severity of his mental disorders. As Lindsay sat in my office, he was securely locked up in a mental institution.

I suspected that she might be considering a divorce or legal separation or wondering if she had a "scriptural" right to do this. Or maybe she was questioning her husband's deranged theology and wanted to compare it to the church's views.

"How can I help?" I asked.

Her eyes moistened. "The doctors—well, they say he isn't responding to treatment—won't even talk to them. He insists he's a great man of God, and he doesn't have a problem; they're the ones who are crazy. I finally get to visit him next month; it's been almost a year since I've seen him. . . ." The tears increased and her voice broke. "I keep thinking . . . well, I wonder . . . *will he still love me? What will I do if he doesn't?*"

WHAT DO YOU BELIEVE?

If you have fallen into the victim role over and over, you might need to take a scrupulous look at your beliefs about trust and your patterns of trusting. What makes you decide to trust a man? Charm, understanding, good looks? Do you quickly trust someone who treats you kindly or makes you feel good? In trust, especially when personal safety is concerned, *charm counts for little*. Character is what matters. You cannot evaluate character in an instant; it takes time.

Trust is earned. Blind trust isn't noble. Blind trust or just deciding, "I don't really know this man but . . . oh well, forget the doubts; I'm going to trust him" may feel courageous, even adventuresome. It could be just stupid!

Nowhere in Scripture does it say women ought to trust everybody. It warns us to the contrary, emphasizing the foolishness of placing trust too readily. Even within the church, we must earn each other's trust:

"Deacons . . . are to be men worthy of respect, sincere, not indulging in much wine, and not pursuing dishonest gain. . . . They must first be tested; and then if there is nothing against them, let them serve as deacons" (1 Tim. 3:8,10).

Early church leaders warned about people who should not be trusted, no matter how charming or spiritual they appeared: "But mark this: There will be terrible times in the last days. People will be lovers of themselves, lovers of money, boastful, proud, abusive, disobedient to their parents, ungrateful, unholy, without love, unforgiving, slanderous, without self-control, brutal, not lovers of the good, treacherous, rash, conceited, lovers of pleasure rather than lovers of God—having a form of godliness but denying its power. *Have nothing to do with them*" (2 Tim. 3:1-5 italics added).

Like Ted Bundy, unscrupulous men found it easy to win women's trust:

"They are the kind who worm their way into homes and gain control over weak-willed women, who are loaded down with sins and are swayed by all kinds of evil desires, always learning but never able to acknowledge the truth" (2 Tim. 3:6-7).

These are serious warnings. In some of Paul's letters, he listed the names of those he had found untrustworthy so others would be forewarned. The apostle seemed to think Christians were vulnerable, even gullible. They could be taken in, perhaps because they were such loving and open people.

Even God doesn't ask you to trust him blindly. The message of the Bible is not merely, "Trust God because he is God." The message is more like, "Take a look at God's character. He is both good and dependable. It is safe to trust him."

My trust in God is based on his character. He is not unpredictable, loving me one day and hating me the next. He says what he means and means what he says. No double-talk, no manipulative flattery, no empty promises, and no flowery words. God has integrity. He is truth.

GUIDELINES FOR THE CHRONIC VICTIM

If you are a victim in any sense, the following may help:

1. *Do something about your safety.* If you are in danger of physical abuse, find a place to hide if it comes to that. Keep an extra set of car keys in case of an emergency. Most large cities have shelters and support groups in which abused women help each other find safety.

2. *If you are suffering physical abuse, insist the abuser get help immediately.* Suspect his promises to change. If abuse has happened three times in your marriage, it *will* happen again, unless the abuser receives thorough professional help. Ask your pastor or doctor to suggest places where this help is available. Or contact a Christian counseling agency for recommendations. Your city may also have a domestic violence hotline. You may need to make several phone calls to find the appropriate direction in which to move. In the process, you will discover you are not alone;

support and resources abound to help you and the abusive person.

3. *Let others help you*—your church, family, friends, Bible study group, etc. Build a support system.

Join a prayer group or women's Bible study where you can share your needs and receive encouragement.

4. *Examine your attitudes and beliefs regarding love and trust.* This chapter was designed to help you do that. However, there are whole books dealing with areas we have only touched on, and some of these might be helpful. They are listed at the end of this book (see page 188).

If you are a victim, it is urgent that you not stay one. God does not want you to suffer mistreatment at the hands of others, no matter how much you love those persons. His love will give you the will to value yourself, confront the evil, and courageously follow through until a better relationship has been established.

5
...

The Matriarch

"No child of mine is going to grow up dumb! You will learn to read if I have to beat you every day of your life!"

So little Darcy tried harder. Each day at school she stared at the page until her head ached. The letters were arranged in little groups called words. When she remembered the words, she could read the sentences fluently. But all too often her eyes played tricks on her. Was that letter a *b* or a *d*? If she pronounced "saw" as it appeared to her, she read "was" aloud, and the teacher corrected her. "That's not 'was', Darcy. You know that word. Now just think! S-A-W. How do you sound it out?"

Every day Darcy felt more uncertain and confused. Was the number *six* called *nine*? She would sometimes say sixty-one when the number read sixteen, or sixteen when it read sixty-one. School was hard for the little girl, but she tried to make up for her unpredictable "dumbness" by being good and excelling in "effort." The all-too regular beatings provided motivation. Often she went to school bruised and in pain but determined to do better for her mommy.

The world is now a different place for Darcy. After years of suffering, believing herself dumb, she is joyously alive and feeling increasing hopefulness. Her problem was successfully diagnosed and treated with small doses of medication. Now she hungrily devours every book she gets her hands on!

What about Darcy's mother?

Since her little girl could read normally at times, Darcy's mom knew she was a smart child. So on the days she could not, it was perfectly obvious, Mother said, that she was being stubborn and trying to punish Mom for that last beating. "She *can* do it. She just *won't*!"

Embarrassed and ashamed, Mother kept moving Darcy to different schools. She "forgot" to notify the old school so no incriminating records were sent to the new school. "The problem" was not openly discussed with anyone. It was kept hidden like a horrible, shameful secret.

Darcy coped as well as she could. Besides trying harder, she often attempted to distract attention from her problem by clowning in class. In some schools, the children teased and called her cruel names. In high school, her depression and loneliness became unbearable. Without Mother knowing it, Darcy skipped school more days than she attended, sometimes sitting alone in the park until dismissal time.

When she was grown and the mother of five children herself, Darcy finally discovered that her problems had a physiological basis. She was diagnosed as dyslexic. Her particular kind caused a dysfunction in the inner ear, distorting her vision. Children afflicted with this disorder often feel dizzy, as if they're trying to read in a car, driving along a bumpy road. Their eyes jump off the page, causing them to lose their place—and their concentration.

It's amazing that Darcy is even alive to tell her story. In the later years of her illness, suicide began to seem like a reasonable option. Also amazing is that Darcy, after so many years of hating and blaming her mother, found it in her heart to forgive her. And Mother? She cries when they talk about it. She had believed she was loving her child. "I'm doing this for your good."

Darcy's mother had no doubt been influenced by stories of other parents who, like the father of little Mozart, forced the four-year-old boy to practice piano for hours at a stretch, and sure enough, produced a virtuoso. Plenty of parents fall victim to delusions of power. Hopefully, we see the mistake and back off before we do too much damage. But it is always less than love when we treat our children as computers for which we are to write the programs.

CONTROL

Like the children of many mothers who are perfectionists and controlling of family members, Darcy was an abused child. Not only because she was beaten unjustly, but because her deep needs were not met.

When a loving mother can "always believe in you, always hope, and always think the best," she will persist in getting to the root of a chronic problem such as a learning disability. The love described in the Bible is "not proud, not puffed up." It is not too caught up in the pride of flawless parenting to admit a child has a problem, nor too proud to seek medical or professional help, nor using denial to protect Mother's ego.

Pride may be the real problem when we find ourselves behaving like controlling Matriarchs, bossing everyone around and assuming we know how to attain perfection for everybody's lives. Pride insists you make me look good at all times. Pride believes I must not make the slightest mistake in my parenting assignment. Pride feeds my insecurities, hoping to shore them up by producing perfect kids. Pride is unreasonably embarrassed when evidence sometimes contradicts my shaky facade.

This is not to say parents shouldn't control their children. Of course we must exercise our parental responsibility to appropriately control, correct, and guide our children. The Bible paints a clear picture of genuine parental love, and that picture includes firm discipline, teaching, and even punishment.

The counterfeit we are dealing with here is that *inordinate* need to control that is sometimes labeled love. It manifests itself not only in perfectionistic parents, but in husbands who believe they own their wives and wives who nag and henpeck their husbands.

This need to control arises out of deep insecurity and fear. Rather than trust God's work in our loved ones' lives, we set out to accomplish our own agenda of change. We play Holy Spirit and label our actions love. The label is phony; control is not love.

The Matriarch is overly responsible. She takes on responsibilities that are not rightly hers. I once knew a pastor's wife who made it her duty to see that her husband did his work properly. "Did you remember to call Mrs. Jones today? What are you going to do about the problems with the choir cantata?" Each time the pastor came home for meals, she reminded him of something. "He puts things off," she told me.

Once I was visiting when he stopped by the house to pick up some books. Gwen met him with her list. "Mrs. Saddlewide called, Dear. She wants to know if you've gotten around to visiting her aunt yet—the one who broke her hip? And would you please, Dear, not forget about that list of visitors for Nancy? She really needs it."

"Dear" behaved most patiently and politely in return, saying, "Yes, yes" to all her reminders as he tried to get out the door. Didn't he just want to scream, "Get off my back! I'm capable of doing my job!"

I also understood how Gwen may have slipped into the role of reminder to her husband. Before Jerry and I entered the ministry, my father-in-law gave me advice that saved me a great deal of stress. A pastor himself, he told me, "People will call your house and ask you to tell the pastor this or that for them. From the very first phone call, say, 'Let me give you the number for his office. He'd be glad to talk with you.'

"If you don't intend to be the unpaid co-pastor," he instructed me, "don't take on the pastor's responsibilities."

CHRISTIAN VIRTUES

Women who slip into matriarchal thinking are not inferior. They are usually sensitive, caring, dutiful, hardworking, and dependable. These are all Christian virtues. But these virtues, carried across the boundaries of personal responsibility, come across as meddling, bossing, or nagging.

If you are a conscientious woman, and it bugs you when someone fails to get things done quickly, I prescribe a strong dose of Proverbs. It deals with your particular set of strengths and also contains many cogent truths about the nagging woman.

Remind yourself how you do and do not want to treat family members. Proverbs describes the foolish woman who tears down her house with her hands. It advises men that it's better to live in a corner of the rooftop than in the same house with a quarrelsome wife. It contrasts conversation that encourages and builds up others with words that cut and wound.

If you have a tendency to nag, memorize some of these verses. Or write them on note paper and put them in places like your purse or family bulletin board where you will see them often.

THE WORST FAULT

Psychologist Lewis Terman once studied more than fifteen hundred marriages. When asked to name the worst fault a wife could have, husbands ranked nagging as number one. The Gallup Poll revealed the same thing in another study. Similarly, Mrs. Dale Carnegie has observed,

Nagging causes more unhappiness in families than extravagance, infidelity and poor housekeeping all put together. Yet wives have been trying to influence husbands by nagging for centuries. Legend reports that Socrates spent his time philosophizing under the plane trees of Athens to escape his shrewish wife, Xanthippe. Such differing personalities as Napoleon III of France and Abraham Lincoln were afflicted by nagging spouses. Augustus Caesar divorced his second wife, Scribonia, because, as he himself wrote, he was "unable to put up with her shrewish disposition." Women are still trying to make nagging pay off. To date, it hasn't worked . . . except in reverse.

TOO MUCH MOTHERING

Motherhood's positive qualities are exaggerated in the Matriarch. She mothers too much, too long, or with the wrong people. Husbands don't like to be mothered. They like to be nurtured, loved, and given affection, but not condescendingly, as though you're saying, "You're such a cute little boy; Mommy likes to take care of you, and you need her so much." Or "You're so incapable of doing anything for yourself, I just have to do it all for you."

It's possible to give children too much "mothering." We need to listen to their natural urges to become more capable and independent. As my own sons are growing into young men, they often say, "I know how to do that, Mom." Or "I'm a big boy, Mom."

It's not that they don't need me. But they don't want to be treated like babies. They want it recognized that they are becoming more adult, more capable, and more responsible. Believe me, I wouldn't want it any other way! This is normal, healthy growth.

Sometimes they tell me about pitiful incidents involving the neighborhood boys. "His mom ran out on the football field when he got hurt. Promise me, Mother, that you'll *never* do that if I get hurt!"

I suspect they have exaggerated some of the stories for my benefit. But I get the point when I hear that Carey's mother, holding onto her boy, demanded the baseball coach give her son the pitching honors.

"I'd be *sooo* embarrassed if Mom did that," one of my sons said. And I assured them I consider them much too grown-up to treat them like babies, especially in front of their friends.

We don't always know when we're mothering too much. Some children are not as vocal as mine, and some husbands, like Gwen's, hold their tongue even when they feel smothered or bossed around. They're too nice for their own good! These husbands could enjoy a more pleasant marriage if they found a way to nicely yet firmly say, "Honey, when you do that (nag, remind, smother, etc.), I feel as though you don't think I'm an adult," or "I feel like you're trying to mother me instead of just being my sweetheart and friend."

GOOD REASONS

The Matriarch has valid reasons, in her mind, for controlling. They are usually good reasons on the surface. "It's for your own good" is her mindset. "I'm doing what's right for you." A strong sense of duty is the positive component of her attitudes; the negative component is a need to control.

All of us have a certain need to control our lives. I like to feel that I'm on top of things. Attacking the stack of mail and memos on my desk and reducing it to items marked "done" pleases me. But people, unlike paperwork, have their own agendas. They will not cooperate with our attempts to organize, analyze, and fix. The day will never come when I can attach the note "done" on a person.

QUESTIONS TO ASK YOURSELF

Attempts to control people will destroy your relationships. If you need to control, consider the following:

1. *Do I believe that a person who changes to meet my specifications will be a better person?*

This is a dangerously arrogant belief. Only God knows what would make your husband a better person. He is the only one who has the right to define wholeness and set the standard for what another should become.

2. *Do I feel responsible to make another adult do what he should do?*

3. *Am I playing Holy Spirit?*

If you're trying to control someone who's a believer, the Holy Spirit is already at work in that person enacting change from the inside out. His agenda may be different than yours. You may actually be working at cross purposes to the Holy Spirit.

CHANGING PEOPLE THROUGH INTERCESSION

Several years ago, a small group of women met for an hour weekly to pray for me. "Thanks," I responded when one of them told me about it. "I can use all the prayer I can get."

Later, she described a strange, mystical vision one of them had during prayer time. I was too busy to take it very seriously. However, I began to notice that each time one of these ladies approached me at church, it was to relay another "message from God."

As I thought about it, I realized this was their way of saying God had revealed that something was wrong with me.

These women, I heard via the grapevine, were dabbling in weird doctrines that had to do with demons, spirits, and a super-spiritual, trance-like prayer for the people they wanted to change. Intercession is a biblical word, but they had a screwy definition of it. First, they pleaded with God on behalf of the person who needed change, for example, a husband, child, friend, or pastor. If they persevered and "broke through," the Holy Spirit gave them the gift of discerning of spirits, and they would suddenly discern which demon spirit was causing the problem. Then they could cast out that problem spirit.

Now I understood why I felt uncomfortable around these ladies and why they seemed frustrated with me. I never asked what demon they were working so hard at casting out of me, but I don't think their prayers ever accomplished the desired results!

Whatever change they wanted in me was not even close to where the Holy Spirit was actually working. During that time, a great deal of change *was* happening in me, and I could see his inner work daily. None of the pray-ers knew me, however, so they didn't see the evidences of his work in my life.

Prayer is not a means to control people. Nor is it a means to control God. We will feel frustration and disappointment if we use prayer to call the shots on our loved ones' decisions. Our prayers will betray us to the people we pray for with such ulterior motives.

"I'm praying for you" should never be a subtle way of saying, "I know what's best for you, and I'm telling God how he ought to change you so that you'll be the person I want you to be." Nor should it mean, "You are so incompetent, disappointing, and imperfect I can hardly stand it; I'm going to nag God until he does something about you!"

4. *Do I assume I would be happier if the other person changed?*

Marge longed for her husband Richard to be more romantic. "I love you, Marge" was the best he could do. No ardent phone calls or flowery, passionate love poems about how desirable and beautiful she was.

Richard was a successful accountant and fit the stereotype: practical, accurate, intelligent, stable, dependable, and responsible. Marge fussed and fumed about the lack of romance in her life; if only she had married a romantic man!

One day Richard did not come home from work. He was killed in a freak car accident. It took Marge a long time to recover from the loss of her husband. She had loved him dearly, romantic or not. But after a few years, she carefully ventured into the world of singles and dating.

One "date" was with an artist and a poet. Talk about romance! Marge fell for Branden before the end of the first date. He endeared her to himself with words about her beauty. She received flowers, love notes, and heart-warming phone calls. They went on walks in the rain and trips to the beach.

She and Branden savored sunsets, candlelit restaurants, picnics beside the stream, hikes in the forest—everything romantic she had ever dreamed of doing. They talked of marriage; Branden couldn't wait. But Marge had to consider her teenage children and didn't want to rush it. Their romance continued for more than a year. Then Marge broke it off.

"This romantic man," she told me, "is everything my husband was not. He did the things—almost *all* the things—I always begged God to get Richard to do. I fell in love so hard. Maybe I still love him, I don't know. But I sure don't want to marry him."

"Why not?" He sounded so perfect, after all, and having fallen so deeply in love, I was surprised at her decision.

"He's so *emotional!* He's impulsive and unpredictable. He's too sensitive and always crying over some stupid thing. I couldn't handle being married to a man like that. I like stability and serenity. Someone more solid."

Then she let the tears out. "I want Richard back! Oh God, why didn't I appreciate him when he was alive? Why did I waste all those years trying to change him? I should have enjoyed him when I had the chance!"

The misconception about romantic love that Marge discovered too late: *If I pray hard enough, maybe God will change my husband in the ways I believe would make him more romantic to me.* If God had answered Marge's prayers, she'd still have not come a step closer to the romance she wanted. Marge's focus on Richard's deficiencies kept her from seeing that her way of relating was *destroying* romance.

Some women would be wise to stop praying for their

husbands. At least for awhile. Their ways of praying are exaggerating a faulty focus. Of course, if your husband is *asking* for prayer and support in a difficult time, do pray.

But the prayers that are unhealthy are those which attempt to get God to change another person so that I'll feel more in control and more comfortable; prayers that arise out of the illusion I know what maturity looks like in someone else.

5. *Do I have emotional needs that I try to meet by exerting power over others?*

Do you fear others may hurt you if you do not maintain firm control of the relationship? Do you fear vulnerability or being mistreated? Are you afraid of feeling victimized or helpless? Do you worry that something terrible may happen to you or someone you love?

Sometimes our fears are reasonable and specific. As a child, you almost drowned once; now you're afraid of water or of your child being near water. Many of us cope with these fears by over-controlling. We may feel like we're handling fear, but our over-compensation damages our relationships.

We can find a better way of dealing with our emotional needs than to dominate or control others. If you have trouble understanding yourself and why you are controlling, many resources are available to you.

For example, if you grew up in a dysfunctional family, such as children of alcoholics do, you can learn a lot about yourself through attending a support group sponsored by Adult Children of Alcoholics (ACOA). Many groups meet in churches; perhaps your church offers one on a weekly basis.

Peers in a support group can help you see why you began to relate to people in a controlling way and how those reasons no longer apply to your situation. God uses people to encourage and enlighten us along the way so he can remove the pain and guide us in a positive direction.

6. *Am I over-protective of people I love?*

Do your kids often say, "Quit trying to protect me"? Does your husband remind you, "I can handle it. You don't need to do anything!"

A fine line exists between responsible mothering and over-protection. We cross that line many times in the process of raising children. We may not even know we crossed it. But if we take note of our family's responses, it won't become the norm. If they complain about our smothering them, that's a clue to back off.

LOVE IS NOT CONTROL

The Bible forbids us to be dominating, no matter how good our reasons or deep our emotional needs. Jesus pointedly talked to his followers about the human tendency to place one person over another; that is, the superior and inferior. Jesus said, "You know that those who are regarded as rulers of the Gentiles lord it over them, and their high officials exercise authority over them. Not so with you. Instead, whoever wants to be first must be slave of all" (Mark 10:42-44).

So! It is not our right to boss people around. Philippians 2:1-8 presents the way for us to relate in Christ:

If you have any encouragement from being united with Christ, if any comfort from his love, if any fellowship with the Spirit, if any tenderness and compassion, then make my joy complete by being like-minded, having the same love, being one in spirit and purpose. Do nothing out of selfish ambition or vain conceit, but in humility consider others better than yourselves. Each of you should look not only to your own interests, but also to the interests of others.

Your attitude should be the same as that of Christ Jesus: Who, being in very nature God, did not consider equality with God something to be grasped, but made himself nothing, taking the very nature of a servant, being made in human likeness. And being found in appearance as a man, he humbled himself and became obedient to death—even death on a cross!

This description leaves no room for controlling, commanding, or ruling over another person.

CONTROL POLLUTES LOVE

The desire to grow into a responsible adult is mature and godly. The desire to exert power over other adults is not. To the degree that my love is tinged with desire to control, it is not real love. Part of what I feel is love, but the need to control is an intruder and pollutant of that love.

Can we repent from controlling? Whether control is practiced through nagging, over-protection, playing Holy Spirit, dominating a person's thoughts and choices, or physical punishment such as Darcy's mother used, it is wrong. It is sin. God offers forgiveness and cleansing and a better way to love the people in our lives.

6

...

The Romantic

The Romantic is in love with the emotions of falling in love. She is hooked on these powerful feelings just as a heroin addict is hooked on his drug. Physical cravings motivate the heroin addict; emotional cravings motivate the Romantic. Life is measured in terms of thrills. Compared to the heady excitement of falling in love, all other satisfactions seem bland. Normal life is dull.

This woman has had mostly pleasant experiences with love. She has not felt the deep pain of rejection or a broken heart. Unlike one who stays in a faltering relationship, she is well-protected from the wounds and bruises of love. When excitement wanes and feelings pale, she's gone, singing to herself, "You just can't get the feelings back."

Of course, some Romantics do persist through heartbreak, trying to recapture earlier feelings. They know the pain they risk but carry on the search anyway in their addiction to ecstasy.

HOOKED ON ROMANCE

Drs. Connell Cowan and Melvyn Kinder describe the Romantic as an addict, hooked on romance.

This woman is in love with romance, infatuated with infatuation. She tells the new man in her life that she cares for him, and she truly believes she does. But . . . she is not actually in love with the man but with the rush of love.

As this exquisite high begins to wear off, which it inevitably does when people get to know each other, she feels let down, disappointed, cheated. Instead of viewing this transformation of emotion as a natural phase in the evolution of love, she decides that something must be wrong—either with her capacity to care, which is too scary a thought to consider, or with him, a flaw she hadn't noticed in the beginning.

When Pat met Jerry, she knew this was "it." There had been other "its" in the past, relationships that had all fizzled, but Jerry was different. She couldn't remember feeling this strongly about a man before. This time, she knew it was going to work. Jerry knew how to make her feel wanted and womanly. As Pat recalls, "He was so expressive—much more so than most other men. He did all those **nice things,** like bringing me flowers—he even used to write me poems. I know it sounds corny, but it felt **good.**" But after a couple of months, as the flush of newness faded, Pat began to have gnawing doubts and feelings of disappointment. What was, in fact, simply the end of infatuation she mistook for the end of love—

again. "I guess as we got to know each other better he relaxed a bit—the poems became fewer, and instead of candles . . . and an intimate dinner, Jerry was . . . likely to suggest catching a ball game on TV."

The minor flaws which she once thought made Jerry all the more charming and endearing now became monstrously magnified in her eyes, and she felt herself slowly but surely losing feelings for him.[1]

SWEPT AWAY

Carol Cassell writes about "one of a woman's most pervasive fantasies of being Swept Away by the man of her dreams. Fireworks explode, waves pound, knees buckle, two hearts beat as one. It's embedded in our culture, this notion of the thrilling ecstasy of passion. You can see it everywhere: in songs, movies, literature, advertising."[2]

She claims that addiction to romance "is a tactic, employed unconsciously by women to get what they want— a man, sexual pleasure—Swept Away is, consequently, a counterfeit emotion, a fraud, a disguise of our true erotic feelings which we've been socialized to describe as romance."[3]

This writer points out the damaging effects of this idea that a woman has found true love just because a man has swept her off her feet. She cites instances of all the women who feel used, worthless, and disillusioned the "morning after." She points out the unplanned pregnancies resulting from the irresponsible behavior of women who feel swept away. But Cassell seems to draw cynical conclusions about romance and sex. However, I believe romance is real, good, and something we can enjoy *without* being swept away into stupid choices.

The desire to be "swept away" is common to single and

married women. Romance addicts come in both categories. Sometimes married romantics are too quick to conclude romance has died, and they must find it again somewhere else. Preoccupation with romance works against achieving the qualities that spark romance in a marriage.

WHEN ROMANCE DIES

Tiffany and Brad were married on a cloud of romance. Both were deeply committed to God and to each other. Brad was a good man, the kind who remembered every anniversary, noticed every new hairdo, and was attentive to his wife and family. He was ambitious, successful in his work, and admired in the community. Yet after ten years of marriage, Tiffany struggled with overwhelming self-condemnation and guilt.

"I just don't feel love for him anymore," she said sadly. "I don't know why! Even when he takes me out to dinner or buys a gift . . . I should feel *something!* What's wrong with me?"

Berating herself didn't bring the feelings she "ought" to have, so Tiffany tried prayer. Maybe God needed to teach her more about loving. Or did he want her to give up trying and let him recreate a new love—miraculously? Did other wives have this difficulty? Did God give special grace to love like a good wife should? Maybe God wasn't concerned about romance or her desires to be romantically loved.

As the years passed, Tiffany became even more discouraged. She began to wonder what was wrong with her. Why hadn't God answered her prayers? Was he angry with her because of her lack of feelings toward her husband?

Tiffany's view of herself became troubled with self-doubt. She wondered if she possessed some horrible character defect that made her an unloving person. Was she incapable of deep love? Now she wondered if she were really a Christian, after all. How could she claim she loved God if she felt no love for her husband?

Meanwhile she continued to participate in church and in her children's school activities. At school she met Larry, a single parent who worked nights and often helped out with school events during the day. He became an understanding friend. Although neither meant to become sexually involved, their relationship turned into an affair.

Now Tiffany felt even more guilty. But in her repentance and sorrow, her prayers took a new direction: "God, how can I feel so loving toward Larry when I'm such a failure in loving my husband? Larry doesn't even buy me gifts or flowers or dinners! Why can't I feel these feelings for the right man?"

In time God showed her why. In essence, he said, "You do love Brad and are deeply committed to him. You admire and respect him. But you have felt anger toward him for a long time. You've built a huge dam out of your anger, and that dam blocks the flow of love."

Tiffany described her years of marriage as mostly peaceful. Early on, she had learned not to fight with Brad. He couldn't stand to lose, and she would end up crying for days afterward. She kept quiet when she disagreed and didn't defend herself when he complained about something she did. For more than ten years, he yelled at her whenever he felt like it.

Tiffany reacted to Brad's constant criticism as any normal woman would. She hurt. She felt anger. Sometimes she took it; other times she left the room shortly after the yelling began. Often, she smiled sweetly and pretended it didn't bother her. It did.

As Tiffany began to realize how much Brad's yelling

and criticizing hurt her, the angry feelings she had repressed for so long surfaced. These emotions of rage frightened this woman who had always been too "nice" for anger. But with reassurance that this was part of God's healing process, she allowed herself to feel them. Her angry feelings weren't only toward Brad, but also toward herself.

She was disgusted with herself for being afraid to stand up to her husband, for not letting him know how strongly his tantrums affected her.

NOT A FAVOR

Tiffany wasn't loving her husband when she stood there and patiently "took it." She wasn't doing him any favors with her silent "submission." She didn't even give him the chance to relate in a better way.

It's not surprising that Tiffany mistakenly thought love was absent. She confused love with romantic emotions. The truth is romantic feelings cannot survive in a relationship dominated by tension. Relaxation is essential to romance. Nervousness, fear of saying the wrong thing, defensiveness, and self-consciousness are all enemies of romance.

Tiffany was fortunate; her marriage survived. Brad displayed genuine Christian character when he forgave his wife and honestly faced his own bad habits. He eventually stopped yelling at her, became kind and considerate of her needs, and she fell more deeply in love with him than ever before.

If you identify with Tiffany in any way or suspect that you're addicted to romance, the following nine suggestions may help:

1. *Be realistic about what you can and can't have in this life.*

When we moved to Seattle, I was delighted to discover squirrels living in the tall firs of our yard. *Friendly little things*, I thought, as they learned to eat out of my hand, sometimes coming into the house to receive our offerings of nuts and crackers. Then Maxwell came to live with us. Maxwell is our cuddly, adorable, affectionate English bulldog. He wouldn't hurt a flea let alone a squirrel. But our little friends took one look at that big, square frame with all the loose skin and triple chins and made a snap decision: they no longer wanted a relationship with the Cook family.

Nowadays we miss seeing them on the patio or kitchen floor. But we'd still choose Max. You can't have it all in this life. Every choice we make involves giving up something. Today's women tend to operate under the assumption that they *can* have it all, and they wear themselves out trying. Their elusive quest of too many goals at once leads to disillusionment and regret. Especially in romance.

John Powell points out this attitude as contrary to Christianity:

> Making a commitment to permanent, unconditional love will mean for me that certain experiences, which might otherwise have been mine, are now impossible for me. The man who chooses one woman for his wife and life partner by his very choice has eliminated all other women as possible wives and life partners. It is this very elimination that frightens us on the brink of commitment. Every commitment is like every moment of life: there is a birth and a death in every moment. Something is and something else can never be again. There is a choice and a surrender, a "yes" and a "no."[4]

If I believe I can have it all on this earth, I may live impulsively, failing to weigh my choices. Doing what I feel like doing, grabbing all the gusto I can get, will produce only momentary satisfaction. Meanwhile I cancel out all possibility of getting what I really want. Any rational person can see it is wiser to make considered choices rather than impulsive ones. This means I must identify what is most important to me so that I can distinguish between my values and my emotions. The principle holds whether you are single or married.

2. *Make it a habit to act not on the basis of your emotions, but on the basis of your values.* If you are one who tends to act impulsively, practice making deliberate choices.

"If it feels good, do it" was a popular cliche in the '70's. Many lively girls who lived by that maxim are stuck with the penalties of their spontaneity today. Some contracted incurable herpes and other sexually transmitted diseases. They must live their adult lives with irreversible reminders of their poor choices. They *don't* teach their daughters, "If it feels good, do it."

Your emotions are never a command to act, nor do they always reflect reality. They reveal your perceptions of the facts. Not the facts themselves. Get the facts, then decide!

3. *Examine the values of your life.*

Be specific. Your general values don't change, such as maintaining a relationship with God, living a Christian life, or being honest. But some values change with the seasons of life and dictate our choices.

For example, a young wife who becomes pregnant adjusts her values to accommodate the new life inside her. She will have a different set of values than her friends who aren't parents. A diabetic woman places a high value on her health, regulating her diet, and insulin.

Romance is a wonderful experience. But romance is not the highest value. People who sacrifice everything else for the experience of romance usually regret that sacrifice. At times, a woman is likely to place too much emphasis on her need for it and make herself vulnerable to foolish choices. Some single women dream of a handsome Prince Charming who will sweep them off their feet. They jump too quickly; they fall too fast. Character is more important than charm, especially if you want a romance that will last.

4. *Examine your beliefs about romance in light of the Bible's teachings.*

The most romantic words ever written are found in the Bible. Much of the time, romantic love illustrates God's feelings for his children. The following verse, for example, rings a bell with any woman who's had a truly romantic relationship:

"As a bridegroom rejoices over his bride, so will your God rejoice over you" (Isa. 62:5).

It's thrilling when someone feels that way about you, isn't it? From adolescence, girls look forward to their wedding day. It isn't just the idea of wearing a beautiful gown in a church decked with flowers and candlelight. It's the dream that a wonderful man will watch her come down that aisle, a man who thinks she's so terrific, he wants to share his whole life with her, even if he lives a hundred years.

God understands this yearning. It's a natural desire we have for someone to treasure us. His feelings for you are just that strong, as intense and pleasurable as the feelings of the most adoring groom who ever fell in love.

Hosea used romantic word pictures to tell us about God's love:

91

I will betroth you to me forever; I will betroth you in righteousness and justice, in love and compassion. I will betroth you in faithfulness, and you will acknowledge the Lord. "In that day I will respond," declares the Lord—"I will respond to the skies, and they will respond to the earth; and the earth will respond to the grain, the new wine and oil, and they will respond to Jezreel. I will plant her for myself in the land; I will show my love to the one I called 'Not my loved one.' I will say to those called 'Not my people,' 'You are my people'; and they will say, 'You are my God' " (Hos. 2:19-23).

In biblical days, parents arranged their children's marriages. Marriage was a practical contract and not necessarily expected to become a romantic relationship.

Women did not have equal rights in those days; wives were considered their husbands' property, rather than lovers or friends. Modern people can hardly imagine this; we pay such intense homage to romantic love that it seems almost a crime to marry without it. Our idea that marriage should include emotional intimacy as well as physical didn't exist in their value system.

Jewish women were better off than those in surrounding countries because of certain provisions in the law of Moses. Still, they were expected to earn society's respect by producing babies and pleasing their husbands. It was considered a terrible disgrace to be single or childless. Falling in love was a minor consideration in comparison to these values. Top values for women were being married and having children.

In spite of these conditions, couples experienced romance. Isaac and Rebekah appear to have fallen in love even before their marriage. Most couples who fell in love did so *after* marriage—often their first conversation together took place on their wedding night.

Relationships between men and women took a downward tumble during the generations after the Fall. God's original intentions were nearly forgotten. Jesus referred to these original intentions during a discussion of marriage and divorce. "It was not this way from the beginning," he said, commenting on why Moses had allowed divorce.

"Haven't you read . . . that at the beginning the Creator 'made them male and female,' and said, 'For this reason a man will leave his father and mother and be united to his wife, and the two will become one flesh'? So they are no longer two, but one. Therefore what God has joined together, let man not separate" (Matt. 19:4-6).

What was it like in the beginning? Adam and Eve probably had the best romance ever. They experienced no self-consciousness, no guilt, no shame, no critical comparisons, no fear, and no lack of commitment to stress their love. Until sin entered, they had everything needed for a perfect love affair with none of the romance-destroyers that beset us today.

Although they sinned and romance nearly disappeared, the Bible never lost sight of it. Nearly every book refers to romance and its pleasant emotions. The symbol "the bride" appears often as God's picture of how he wants to relate to his people. Then, all history will climax in a wedding to end all weddings; the marriage of the Lamb. Jesus Christ is the bridegroom, completing the union with his church, the bride of Christ. We return to the relationship the original bride and groom experienced in the garden.

5. Recognize the dangers of romance.

Romance is good. You need not repent of or feel guilty about your romantic desires. Romance, like every other good thing in life, is only dangerous when out of balance or used as an excuse to harm others.

Remember Margret, the presidential secretary who was seduced into stealing secrets for the spy? She's in jail for treason; the judge couldn't let her off just because she pleaded, "But I was in love!" "In love" *feels* like an adequate rationalization for almost anything. But we value our "in love" feelings too highly if we mistake them as a valid reason to:

1. Commit a crime
2. Act against our standards and values
3. Sin
4. Engage in behavior that endangers our own or our families' health or safety
5. Break our marriage commitment
6. Move away from relationship with God
7. Use others to give us love "feelings" instead of loving others for their own sake.

At times, romantic feelings may seem like an acceptable reason to break our marriage vows, but they are not. Romantic feelings may lead to marriage commitment, but then commitment, if it means anything at all, must withstand any subsequent romantic feelings that challenge it. People in love stay together, not so much out of commitment, but because they enjoy each other. Commitment is for the periods we don't feel "in love." And for the times we have romantic feelings for someone else.

6. *Understand the progression of romantic emotions.*

A group of professionals studied romantic relationships for five years at Berkeley Therapy Institute. They observed three stages couples move through:

STAGE I: FALLING IN LOVE

This stage is characterized by warm, exciting emotions.

The couple radiates with the joy of just being together. Stage I enhances all your good feelings about yourself. Self-esteem hits an all-time high. Someone finds you entrancing, desirable, and worthy of endless attention. You are temporarily lifted out of your self-doubt and believe you are the genuinely lovable person he sees.

Both partners are perceived as almost godlike; their faults and vices seem either minuscule or unimportant to each other. "Stage I fosters trust; trust fosters intimacy. Susan said, 'Always before, I felt I had all kinds of things inside me I could never let out. With Murray I feel like I can be completely open. I'm not scared with him. Anything that happens is okay, because there's nothing I have to hold in.' "[5]

In this fairy tale, heady stage of love, we are eager to give anything to make the beloved happy. We give without being asked, without resentment, or without feeling put upon. It's easy to indulge his weaknesses, forgive, and forget. "Getting your own way" is a thought that rarely crosses your mind as you seek to enjoy each evening you spend together. It seems no sacrifice to give up your plans to do something he enjoys.

When they are falling in love, people are deeply responsive to each other's needs. They offer each other unequivocal backing, and display an inexhaustible interest in each other's feelings. . . . Both partners strive to be their finest selves. They feel so good about themselves and about the relationship they're tempted to believe that the relationship will realize their fantasies and transform their lives. . . . But the bleak fact is that Stage I is necessarily fleeting. Over time, satiation dilutes the intense pleasure the partners originally found in being together. Real-world obligations encroach on the relationship. As evidence of each other's shortcomings piles up and as the relationship begins to exact visible cost, mutual idealization gives way to mutual disillusionment.[6]

It's easy to fall in love. But falling is not all there is to love. The Romantic forgets that other stages are inevitable in the building of a lasting love. She only labels love a relationship as intense as Stage I. Her definition is flawed.

STAGE II: MUTUAL DISAPPROVAL

Stage II tests all the foundations built in Stage I. The same faults that seemed so unimportant then now appear as giant defects. The prince is a frog after all! Hidden expectations surface, and neither partner can meet the other's agenda.

One couple put it, "We're constantly at each other's throats. The things that would have caused little fights between us have gotten way out of hand, and we're having huge screaming battles."[7] Some experts call this stage "The Storming."

Whereas Stage I gave unlimited admiration, Stage II brings mutual disapproval and feelings of rejection. This sounds as though romance can't last, but the truth is genuine love can endure.

Stage II forces us to work out the implications of our commitment to love one another. Anybody can love when the feelings are intense and compelling. Remember, people who feel "in love" don't need a commitment to stay together. Commitment is the earnest money we put down guaranteeing we will hang in there and keep loving when the feelings are miserable, just as we kept loving when it felt good. Couples who deal with Stage II in a Christian fashion have a joyous future ahead.

STAGE III: SECURE LOVE

Stage III brings the enjoyment of real, proven, secure love between two people who have recognized each other's faults and come to terms with them. They have decided to love each other with the full awareness that it is not all warm fuzzies and poetic beauty. Stage III does not have the emotional intensity of Stage I, but it is every bit as pleasurable. Romantic love grows and flourishes in a way only possible for those who have experienced the disillusionment and necessary eye-openings of Stage II.

7. *Don't give up too soon!*

During Stage II, many couples turn to divorce or affairs as a solution. They use the new person as the cure for lost romance in their marriage, but this romance will also meet Stage II; the lovers will have to walk through the same territory they ran away from in the last relationship. Some lovers lack the courage, and they spend their lives running away!

8. *Be willing to build.* To experience lasting romance, you must *build* a relationship over time that involves richer, more satisfying meanings than the fantasy world of early love. You must believe that the satisfaction found at the end of these stages is even keener than the thrill of falling in love.

After twenty-seven years of marriage, Jerry and I enjoy a relationship that is much better than the first years of falling in love. Nobody could have convinced us back then that we would experience fuller joys ahead or pleasures we could not imagine. Later, during our own Stage II, we seriously doubted there were any joys ahead! Now we look back on those struggles as valuable in producing the growth and acceptance of one another that led us to Stage III.

9. *Create romantic love in your marriage.*

I teach a session in marriage seminars entitled, "Romantic Love." It addresses how to stay in love. I refer to long-term studies and discuss the elements found in relationships where romantic love endures.[8]

Lasting romantic love is not produced by Cupid's arrow or a mystical zap from heaven. It is something you can choose to put into your marriage.

The feelings are a result of practical behavior: treating one another with respect, admiration, interest, kindness, enthusiasm, encouragement, support, and understanding. Biblical *agape* love is closely tied to the causes of romance. Lasting romance is made up of Christian love coupled with admiration, friendship, and physical attraction between a man and woman. A good example of this is the poetic Song of Solomon—a delightful picture of romantic love.

When I studied the results of secular studies designed to reveal the "causes" of romantic love and then studied the teachings of the Bible, I was impressed with the similarity. Again, science has caught up with the ageless wisdom of Scripture! Romance was not magic all along, it was just one expression of the love described in the Bible centuries ago.

If you are a romantic woman, this is all good news for you. Your best hope of having the long-lasting romantic love you yearn for is found in a Christian marriage where commitment is secure and two people are willing to build into their relationship the elements which produce romance.

If you are single, keep these guidelines in mind:

1. *Romance is based on relationship, not possessions, looks, or glamour.* Don't make the mistake of waiting for the perfect romantic man. He doesn't need to look like a

movie star, drive a glamorous car, and wear designer clothes; in fact, these superficials may fool you into thinking he is romantic when actually he is shallow.

2. *Build Christian character, spiritually, socially, and intellectually.* Don't wait for Prince Charming to magically endow you with the capability for romance.

3. *Deal constructively with self-esteem problems.* Don't mourn your defects; build yourself up. Romance will not cure low self-esteem. Romance is most lasting between two adults who *have* healthy self-esteem.

4. *Cultivate friendships with both men and women.*

5. *Don't sit around moaning, "All the decent guys are taken."* This attitude blocks you from seeing people as they really are. If you refuse to relate to any man who doesn't fit the perfect image of romance and glamour shown on movie screens, you are extremely vulnerable to anyone who can fake the image!

6. *Be truthful with yourself about love or you will miss the best pleasures that reality brings.*

Infatuation counterfeits romantic love. As you grow in learning to love as God loves, you will recognize the counterfeit and determine to settle for nothing less than the real thing: a marriage of enduring romantic love where your commitment to God and to each other strengthens and deepens the romance through each stage of growth.

7
...
The Angel

What an elegant, beautiful lady, I thought the first time I met Natalie Winters at the airport. She graciously welcomed me and introduced herself as president of the women's group. In the following days with her group, I became impressed with her talents as well as her loveliness. Natalie was a natural leader and an excellent organizer.

But after a few days, she seemed tired, burned out from too many demands. Not only did she organize and lead the events at which I spoke, she also brought homemade cookies.

"How did you manage to fit baking into your busy schedule?" I asked in amazement.

"Oh, I just got up early this morning," she responded with a laugh.

ASK A BUSY PERSON

At church, Natalie played the organ and served on the board of trustees. "I don't know how the church would get along without Natalie," her pastor said. "She's busy, but she does a bang-up job. Like I always say, if you want something done and done well, ask a busy person! Why last year, she. . . ."

Something clicked inside. I'd heard that remark numerous times but never before wondered about the feelings of a busy person.

As we drove back to the airport, the busy person confided that she wished she were not so much in demand. "I feel guilty if I say no," she said. "I don't want them to think I don't care. Because I do care. But I'd like some time to myself once in a while. Time to enjoy my home or read a book. Or just do something because I *want* to, rather than because *they need me to!* I'm to the point where I'm afraid I'll scream if one more person says, 'We need you to. . . .' "

Many Natalies burn out and quit their good work prematurely because of tiredness or disillusionment. They regard their talents as enemies. They wish they had kept their capabilities hidden. For the purposes of this chapter, we will make a sweeping generalization and call this woman the Angel.

JUST SAY YES

Why do I believe the Angel has bought a counterfeit for love? Simply this: her working definition of Christian love boils down to: *do whatever others ask you to do. Say yes.*

The Angel could benefit from training in refusal skills. However, it's her Christian duty to say yes—emphasis on *Christian*—to be charitable at all times, ever good and helpful, meeting the needs of all who ask her. And do they ask her!

I'LL DO IT

Does busyness equal godliness? The Angel becomes confused if she tries to distinguish the difference. Besides, she is much too busy to meditate on such thoughts. The phone rings with news of another baby born. "Will you be giving a baby shower?" The expected answer: "Yes, of course, I'll do it."

The Angel's list of demands accumulates. Pressures escalate, and she finds herself barely making it from the phone to school, to church, to the committee, to the store, to the tupperware party, and to the children's music lessons.

My husband writes of this kind of busyness in his book *A Few Things I Learned Since I Knew It All.*

The win/lose mentality produced in me a certain grimness that I call the Busy/Important/Serious syndrome. Busy, Important, and Serious hang out together, and they take over the lives of winners.

Surely you have noticed this. Important people are always busy. They rush from somewhere to somewhere else. Wherever they are is typically on the way to where they are going, to some destination which is never quite clear but always more important than here.

It is all very seductive. I am busy because I am important, and I am important because I am busy. It has a certain rush, and intoxication, and excitement. Researchers report that one can actually get high on and become addicted to one's own adrenalin. Living on an adrenalin high leaves me weary, but I don't read that as a warning from my body that something is amiss. Instead, I read my weariness as evidence of heroism; it shows how dedicated I am to Christ and the work of Christ.

"I am so tired," I say to myself, "but I must keep going. I am important, needed." I am also deliciously aware that others are saying with admiration, "He works so hard. How can he possibly accomplish so much? He certainly is a great man of God."

I hear bits and pieces of this, translate it into more evidence of my importance, and slide closer and closer to the precipice. All the while, I think things are as they should be. . . . Then comes the crash. It can take various forms—a body gone on strike, emotions no longer reflecting reality, a marriage in trouble. Now the winner hangs on the brink of becoming—horror of horrors—a loser. "He is certainly a great man of God," is replaced with, "If he were really a man of faith, how could this happen?" Or, "There must have been some hidden sin in his life."

Hidden failings could be responsible, of course, but it's also possible that he has just succumbed to over-load, to the seductive power of Important and Busy, to fatigue. The fatigue I'm talking about has little to do with taking a day off now and then, or going for a long walk on the beach.

There is a tiredness those little respites won't touch. It's the bone-weariness of a never-ending competition that God never called us to enter in the first place. A tiredness whose companions are Busy and Important.

Oh, yes, Serious is the third partner in this devastat-ing and seductive little trio. Like a virus, Serious in-fected my entire being. Fun and spontaneity and life and laughter, feeling unwanted and unwelcome, slipped quietly away.[1]

Jerry's observations are placed in the context of a discussion on success, winning, and losing. If you're not a winner in the game of life, then you must be a loser. The Angel views these issues in spiritual opposites: good or bad, spiritual or selfish, dedicated or uncommitted. In an effort to be "good," habits of constant pleasing develop.

We could speculate as to reasons for inordinate pleasing. Perhaps our parents, desiring obedience, taught us to say yes and never no. But when children grow up—in fact, *if* they are to grow up—they need to learn that no is also a good answer. They must learn to make choices, which means saying no to some things in order to say yes to others.

We could also glibly say the Angel is a people pleaser. She fears criticism or rejection, so whatever the request, she obliges. "What will they think of me?" is constantly in her thoughts. Perhaps. But not always.

Dr. Kevin Leman writes about women in this cycle. He calls them "The Pleasers" and believes they need to take control of their lives, quit "yes-ing" their lives away and move to *NO!* He hears pleasers repeat these common complaints:

"Why can't I say no?"

"I love him too much."

"He's sleeping with another one. . . ."

"I have to walk on eggshells."

He lists six characteristics of a pleaser personality:

1. These women learned to be pleasers when they were little girls.

2. Pleasers often come from unhappy homes in which their fathers gave them very little attention, support, or love.

3. Pleasers are willing to settle for small favors.

4. The key characteristic in almost all pleasers: low self-esteem.

5. They try to keep everyone happy.

6. Pleasers usually feel inferior to men, or at least have a strong need to be "good girls" so men will approve of them.[2]

The good girl obeys and especially obeys authority figures. If she believes she is inferior to men simply because they are men, she feels guilty not obeying or pleasing all men in her life. This includes co-workers, her husband, other adult men or even her teenage sons.

Dr. Leman notes that pleasers come in different packages. He describes the super-suffering pleaser, the depressed pleaser, the exhausted pleaser, the mildly discouraged pleaser, and lastly, the positive pleaser.

The positive pleaser has achieved a balance between pleasing people and requiring that others treat her respectfully and considerately. She can be:

• assertive without being abrasive
• confident without being cocky
• self-nurturing without being selfish[3]

THE FAULTY BELIEF

These theories fit many of us, but I want to address the belief that pleasing is the most loving way to live as a Christian. This is to live sacrificially to the point it becomes self-destructive.

This Angel is a capable, conscientious woman, not a self-punishing neurotic. She has heard many sermons on denying yourself, sacrificing and serving, yet she still feels guilty that she's not doing more. Each message achieves the desired result; she resolves to try harder.

One Sunday I happened to be in a church where the pastor was preaching from Mark 8: "If anyone would come after me, he must deny himself and take up his cross and follow me" (Mark 8:34).

Some women in the congregation already carried enormous loads. They had gained one quiet hour for worship because salaried nursery attendants cared for their toddlers. Some dealt with the grief of divorce and abandonment while others tried to make ends meet with small salaries and big mortgages. The women's lives were dominated by carpools, kids outgrowing their clothes, baby bottles, laundry, teenagers, part-time and full-time jobs, and hectic activity that never seemed to meet the demands of life.

But the pastor had his own needs. He needed a successful fundraising bazaar to finance enlarging the sanctuary. He needed a few pie socials, more teachers for Sunday school, and. . . .

As I observed the guilt on the faces of these women, I found myself resenting his methods. "Do you *really* love?" he thundered. "If we really cared, there would be more than enough workers for Sunday school—we would never have a shortage. Why do so few take up the cross? Why are most Christians so selfish and self-centered?"

This episode made me appreciate my own church. We refuse to use guilt motivation to obtain volunteers. This refusal is one way we express respect for the congregation. It is wrong to use guilt to manipulate people, even if it is successful in getting new carpet for the building. The end does not justify the means.

Am I saying you should ignore all pleas for help at your church? In your local school? What about the community and your immediate neighborhood? Surely we can't just close our eyes to the needs! No. But we can select the needs on which we will spend our energies. We can learn to say no with a clear conscience.

As I listened to the pastor preach about "taking up the cross," I wondered what Jesus would have said to that group of women. Would he have used these words? "Come to me, all you who are weary and burdened, and I will give you rest. Take my yoke upon you and learn from me, for I am gentle and humble in heart, and you will find rest for your souls. For my yoke is easy and my burden is light" (Matt. 11:28-30).

NO LIGHT BURDEN

Nothing could describe the Angel less than "light-burdened!" She carries the weight of the world on stooping shoulders. Her "yoke" is anything but easy. Often she finds herself accepting tasks that don't fit her aptitudes. The yoke scrapes and chafes, tiring her far sooner than it would tire the person who has the needed aptitudes. Meanwhile, her true desires are laid aside, the desires which more likely fit her abilities.

Perhaps all these responsibilities did not come from God. Could that be why they are breeding nervousness, fatigue, and a growing resentment toward the God whom she feels has doomed her to bear such a difficult "cross"?

God is not to blame for the late-night toiling that often characterizes the Angel. He has nothing against rest! "In vain you rise early and stay up late, toiling for food to eat— for he grants sleep to those he loves" (Ps. 127:2). God wants to make your load lighter, not heavier. He'd never complain if you were caught relaxing.

Sleep loss and heavy burdens come from taking others' expectations too seriously. Often others are not asking for action; they don't intend to increase our loads. They are merely offering suggestions and opinions. It is wise to listen rather than rush into action, concluding prematurely, "I must *do* something."

LISTENING TO PEOPLE

Gordon MacDonald addressed fellow pastors in a seminar. "A minister must be a good listener," he said. "It's important to my work. There are people I must listen to." Following is Gordon's list of people to whom he must listen:

1. God
2. My wife   (She is my partner. She knows me best, shares my life, and understands my goals.)
3. The church   (I cannot minister to their needs if I do not know their needs.)
4. My friends   ("Faithful are the wounds of a friend" [Prov. 27:6 KJV]).
5. My mentors   (Carefully chosen older, wiser, and more experienced godly men who care about me and have agreed to coach me from time to time. "Wisdom is found in those who take advice" [Prov. 13:10]).
6. My children   (They sometimes see the important things before anyone else. They may be God's voice to busy parents.)
7. My critics and my enemies   (They force me to take an honest look at myself. They occasionally reveal a need in me I would not be faced with by my kindhearted friends.)

This list has proven very useful to me. I, too, find it essential to listen and terribly unwise to dash ahead heedless of others' suggestions or input. Respectful listening, however, differs greatly from subservience to the wishes of others. If my Christian duty is reduced to running around tirelessly trying to do all the things other people think I ought to do, then I am sentenced to a life of impossible conflict. And probably an early grave!

Besides that, I have put all these frail humans in the unlikely position of God. Jesus Christ is not Lord of my life at all. My mother is Lord. Or my husband, child, pastor, friends, relatives, supervisor, co-workers, church members, or even worse—my critics and enemies have become the ruling powers of my life.

Let's look more closely at our tendencies to put human beings in the role of Lord. Sometimes they grow out of seeds planted in childhood.

UNRESOLVED ISSUES FROM THE PAST

Author Collette Dowling writes movingly of little girls' needs to please their mothers. She quotes a piece that gave insight into her own relationship with her daughter:

I was the jewel in my mother's crown. She often said, "Maja can be relied upon, she will cope." And I did cope. I brought up the smaller children for her so that she could get on with her professional career. She became more and more famous, but I never saw her happy. How often I longed for her in the evenings. The little ones cried and I comforted them but I myself never cried. Who would have wanted a crying child? I could only win my mother's love if I was competent, understanding and controlled, if I never questioned her actions nor showed her how much I missed her; that would have limited her freedom, which she needed so much.

Then the author adds her own story:

Those words were spoken by a patient of the Swiss psychoanalyst Alice Miller and recorded in her book *Prisoners of Childhood*. When I first read them, they brought back vividly what had happened with Gabrielle. Like Maja, Gabrielle was the oldest child who stayed home with the others while I went off on research trips. She cooked for them, picked up after them, read to them. . . . Gabrielle was the "big girl"—mother's helper, mother's pride. She was the one who listened to my problems, and gave solace and support. I never questioned what was happening, only thought how lucky I was to have such a child, until, in her late teens, Gabrielle rebelled against her deprivation—the loss, in a very real sense, of her childhood. She had been my "special girl," yes, but at the price of never crying, of keeping her hurts and frustrations to herself, of never having me to herself in the evenings because I was always in my office working. Gabrielle was the jewel in her mother's crown, but it was *mother* who was wearing the crown. . . . Did I have real empathy for my child, or was I in fact putting myself first?[4]

When the habit of living to please Mother carries over into adult life, it is particularly unhealthy. Whether Mother was hard to please or overflowing with approval and affection, pleasing her is not an appropriate motivation for living. Either way, a child's motivation is substituting for an adult one.

If in all my relationships, I am constantly asking myself, "What would make Mother happy?" or "What would Mother expect me to do here?" I am in bondage to the habit of pleasing. I end up evaluating my actions and behavior toward friends and acquaintances in the manner I would behave if Mother were present. I can't enjoy these other people for their own sake. In fact, I don't even see them as themselves, but as extensions of Mother whom I must please today.

The same things apply as we strive for the approval of our fathers. The unresolved need to win the approval of a father may focus on a husband or boyfriend. Most women expend far too much energy striving for approval of the men in their lives.

Continual striving for a man to give identity or validation is misdirected effort. No man (or woman) on earth has the power to give you those things. The woman who seeks her efficacy in a man ends up attaching so much importance to his opinions that she replaces God with a fallible human being. This unsuspecting man, who knows himself to be only too human, has no idea that his tastes, opinions, whims, and suggestions are taken far more seriously than he himself would ever take them.

He has no illusions about his superior wisdom or his right to lordship. So he does not comprehend the degree to which his woman overreacts to him. He doesn't realize she has difficulty separating his opinions and directives from God's. She needs a man's approval so badly she even feels guilty going against his desires, half-expecting God to punish her if she does.

What would happen if women placed as much weight on what God thinks as they do on what the men in their lives think? Or if they shifted their focus and value from striving for a man's affection onto living as God created them to live? Not apologetically, tentatively, cautiously checking for male approval before taking a step, then quickly retreating at the slightest frown or raised eyebrow—but confidently making adult decisions.

A woman who places her identity in Christ can be herself without apology. She makes her own decisions and serves others cheerfully. But her service is not servility:

> A great difference separates Christian service from servility. A woman who knows who she is in Christ can never again be obsequious. She cannot pretend she is a nothing; be trampled, walked on, or treated with disdain. Her life will not be spent as a pawn in someone else's chess game. She does not fall prey to those who dominate by intimidation, temper tantrums, or anger. Her knowledge of her own value prevents her from succumbing to such treatment.

Jesus lived a life of service but he was not a pleaser.

Jesus didn't feel demeaned in doing the work of a household servant. He had no uneasy ego to protect, no precarious image to maintain. After his resurrection, he appeared to his disciples one morning when they had taken their boat out on the lake to fish. What was he doing when they spotted him back on shore? Cooking breakfast.

How does this kind of serving differ from the woman described earlier? Why is it not servitude or servility? Here's why; Jesus was not a victim. He chose. He was not used, manipulated, coerced, or trapped at any point, even in his death.

In his discourse on the good shepherd, he said, "No one takes [my life] from me, but I lay it down of my own accord" (John 10:18).

When we choose to use the talents, intelligence, and power God has entrusted to us, we do so not to appease expectations; to get someone off our back; or even worse, to coerce, exploit, and damage others, but to bless them. This is a more genuine serving than that dutiful drudgery put out by the victim. When we, as free agents—strong, valuable, and empowered by God—cheerfully offer our service to others, it is a true choice. Our service is a gift. No mixed motives. No waiting like the obedient puppy for a pat on the head and a few table scraps. We love because it is our nature to love. We choose loving service as the best way to live our lives. Living a life of love is the wise choice of a woman who has accepted her God-given power.[5]

If you are an Angel, you must make a deliberate effort to create time for yourself and your needs.

My friend Idella used to tell our Bible study group, "When I buy a new calendar each year, I color in all the Wednesday mornings. On that day, I come to Bible study for my own needs and to be with my friends. I don't schedule appointments. I don't do the laundry or anything else short of an emergency. That's the time for my needs, and I always feel energized by Wednesday afternoons."

I reached a point in my own life when I realized the days had become too complicated. I was trying to be all things to all people in my desire to be an effective minister. Frustration piled up as each day I failed to meet my expectations. When I took stock of myself, I realized I was trying not to disappoint anybody. I couldn't return all the phone calls that came into my office every day. I felt guilty about the incomplete calls, the unfinished letters, and the people with whom I hadn't *yet* had lunch!

The more I tried to meet all these demands, the heavier the expectations—my own expectations of myself and those of others for me. Then I noticed, quite sadly, that I'd squeezed friendship out of my life in favor of "ministry" and business. My family seemed only another set of demands. Rather than enjoy my children, I regarded them as a "workload."

I will not live this way! I said to myself and to God. I surveyed the contents of my busy life. I would choose my time investments, not according to demand, but according to my values. I made a few commitments to myself and those remain to this day:

1. I will only make commitments I can keep.
2. I will have time for friends.
3. I will leave space in each day for kindness.

At first glance, this looks like a regression into selfishness. Actually, it is a far more loving way to live than the way I had lived. Let me explain these statements.

1. *I will only make commitments I can keep.*

This means I refrain from an automatic yes to every opportunity that arises. I do not believe opportunity only knocks once. I don't believe every opportunity to minister is one I must seize, as if I were the only possible answer to that need. This attitude borders on a Messianic complex.

Sometimes "uncommitted" is a good word. I can't be committed to everyone, every cause, and every need in this world. So why make empty promises and half-felt commitments? Why not devote myself to a few things I care deeply about and give those few things my best energies?

A good answer may be, "No, I can't take on any more commitments just now." You don't need to make excuses like, "I'm so busy because . . . well, I have a toddler, and my husband has been fighting the flu and. . . ." No excuse is needed. You simply aren't taking on more commitments at this time. Few people would receive that as a personal insult. In fact, they will appreciate your directness and honesty.

2. *I will have time for friends.* Often the Angel feels she has few friends. She is always in the role of helping others, focusing on their needs, or listening to their problems.

When she has a crisis of her own, or a down time, you would think the people she's served would come rushing to her aid, wouldn't you?

Chances are, however, they don't know her well enough to be of comfort. She is spread so thin meeting the needs of others, everyone assumes she has no needs of her own.

All of us need to cultivate relationships just for the fun of it. We need friends with whom we can relax. It doesn't always have to be a heavy, serious thing. Those who laugh with us can also cry with us when the need comes. No woman should be so busy "working for the Lord" that she forfeits the joys of friendship. Leo Buscaglia is often known to say, "No one should have to die alone; no one should have to cry alone."

3. *I will leave space in each day for kindness.*

As Christians, the love inside us often bubbles out during a day. Sometimes it surfaces in an urge toward kindness. You have an unbidden thought, "I'd like to take some flowers to Millie," or "I wonder how Dad is feeling today . . . maybe I'll give him a call." We can feel free to act on those urges instead of putting them on our long list of "things I gotta do."

The religious men in the story of the good Samaritan had no time for kindness. They couldn't stop long enough to help a bleeding man. They may have had theological reasons. Or meetings to go to, important spiritual meetings where prayer and worship would take place. Jesus chose the man these fellows would have labeled a sinner to illustrate what loving your neighbor meant. Loving your neighbor is responding to the need that stares you in the face as you walk down the road going about your business.

When an opportunity for kindness popped into my busy, over-committed, tightly scheduled former life, I would grit my teeth and walk on by, just like the priest and Levite. I felt terrible about it.

To solve this situation, I found it necessary to "schedule" blank time in my agenda. My calendar is deemed "full" at a certain point. Some of the "filled up" slots are those padded spaces, the air in which to breathe kindness as the urge or need arises.

These simple rules have worked well for me. I pass them on to all who would live lovingly without running themselves into the ground. The Angels among us are sensitive, gracious women who can beautify the earth for many rich years. So allow yourself to live a long life, Angel! Be as good to yourself as you are to others so that we can enjoy your fragrance for many years to come.

8
...
The Addict

The Addict was once called a "nymphomaniac." Everyone believed her ailment was caused by too many hormones. One such girl lived in our little town. Everyone in the family was a respectable, clean Christian. Except Lucy. Her constant sleeping around embarrassed her parents who were leaders in a fundamentalist church.

It started when she was quite young—around fourteen. "She'll go to bed with anything that wears pants," people said. "Just can't help herself!" A pretty girl, she was compulsive about sex.

Finally Lucy's distraught mother took her to the family doctor who gave the problem a "medical" label. Whatever he suggested the family do about this abundance of hormones was apparently not a success. Lucy's life proceeded from disaster to disaster despite the best efforts of her church, doctor, and parents.

COMPULSIVE SEX

A better word for Lucy today is sexaholic. It applies equally to men who are controlled by compulsive sexuality. The sexaholic may equate sex with love. Or she may have begun with that misconception and progressed to using sex as a pacifier or "fix."

Her sexual experiences are not so much expressions of love as they are of anxiety, discouragement, fear, or loneliness. Whatever the problem, it'll feel better if she gets her fix—sex.

In describing her sense of emptiness, she may say, "I need to be loved," or "I need to be touched and held," or "I need someone to care about me." She needs love but only feels loved if it is expressed in one specific way.

Don't get nervous if you enjoy your sexual life or experience strong sexual desires—you're not neccessarily a sexaholic.

The sexaholic is an addict who uses sex as a narcotic. Sex helps her temporarily escape her tensions or stresses. The normal woman has times of heightened sexual desire, but the sexaholic has a serious emotional disorder characterized by compulsive behavior or feelings of insatiable sexuality.

A recurring line in television scripts: "I need a drink." It goes like this: detective hero or romantic lead enters stage right. He's got a problem, or he just solved one. Either way, his line is "I need a drink." This is careless script writing. It models a damaging attitude; whatever the need, a drink will help!

ONE CURE

Life is like that for the sexaholic. One cure for whatever ails you. One cure for the blues. One cure for self-doubt.

120

One cure for loneliness. Do country singers know how much support they lend to the sexaholic's rationale?

One male sexaholic often said to his wife, "I've got a big meeting to chair this morning so I need to have sex." The wife began to feel his sexuality had nothing to do with her. At times, he would grab her cruelly, and say, "I've had a rough day, and I need it."

The woman with this problem is trapped not by her hormones, but by her misconceptions. She has not learned to cope with life in a healthy way. Her concepts of love are desperately warped. She rationalizes with lines like, "God created sex, why shouldn't I enjoy it?" or "Everybody needs love," or "I only feel loved when I'm having sex; you don't think I ought to live without love, do you?" Sort of like the addict who says, "God created marijuana; why shouldn't I enjoy it?"

Sex *can* be a great source of comfort. God designed it as a pleasure that meets many of a husband's and wife's emotional needs. But normal women understand that sex is not a narcotic, not a cure-all, not a pacifier, not a substitute for facing life squarely and dealing with it courageously. Normal loving in our sexual experience issues from a person-to-person intimacy, never the use or abuse of one person by another.

PASSION IN THE BIBLE

God describes normal sexuality clearly and enthusiastically in the Bible. For example: "May your fountain be blessed, and may you rejoice in the wife of your youth. A loving doe, a graceful deer—may her breasts satisfy you always, may you ever be captivated by her love" (Prov. 5:18-19).

The apostle Paul wrote that a Christian man should not deny his wife sexual fulfillment by claiming spirituality as an excuse. At that time, many ascetic groups associated spirituality with celibacy, and some even *forbade* marriage. Although Paul was single, he made it clear that Christianity was not a celibacy cult:

> The husband should fulfill his marital duty to his wife, and likewise the wife to her husband. The wife's body does not belong to her alone but also to her husband. In the same way, the husband's body does not belong to him alone but also to his wife. Do not deprive each other except by mutual consent and for a time, so that you may devote yourselves to prayer. Then come together again so that Satan will not tempt you because of your lack of self-control (1 Cor. 7:3-5).

God referred to the sexual act in the first chapter of the Bible, where the creation of the human race is described: "So God created man in his own image, in the image of God he created him; male and female he created them. God blessed them and said to them, " 'Be fruitful and increase in number; fill the earth and subdue it' " (Gen. 1:27-28).

In a second, more detailed description, the Bible concludes the story: "For this reason a man will leave his father and mother and be united to his wife, and they will become one flesh" (Gen. 2:24).

The Canticles (Song of Songs) is a poetic and romantic description of two lovers and their feelings and passions. God is not at all embarrassed about sex, nor does he frown when a wife experiences lovemaking with unbridled enjoyment. The women in this lovely bridal poem says things like this:

Let him kiss me with the kisses of his mouth—
for your love is more delightful than wine.
My lover is to me a sachet of myrrh
resting between my breasts.
My lover is to me a cluster of henna blossoms
from the vineyards of En Gedi.
How handsome you are, my lover
    Oh, how charming!
    And our bed is verdant.
Like an apple tree among the trees of the forest
    is my lover among the young men.
I delight to sit in his shade,
    and his fruit is sweet to my taste.
Strengthen me with raisins,
    refresh me with apples,
    for I am faint with love.
His left arm is under my head,
    and his right arm embraces me (Song of Songs 1:2,
    13-14, 16; 2:3, 5, 6).

While the Bible heartily approves the celebration of
sexuality in marriage, it just as heartily warns against the
misuse of sexuality. Here are some of those warnings:

The body is not meant for sexual immorality, but for
the Lord, and the Lord for the body.... Do you not
know that your bodies are members of Christ himself? Shall I then take the members of Christ and
unite them with a prostitute? Never!
    Flee from sexual immorality. All other sins a man
commits are outside his body, but he who sins sexually sins against his own body. Do you not know that
your body is a temple of the Holy Spirit, who is in
you, whom you have received from God? You are not

your own; you were bought at a price. Therefore honor God with your body (1 Cor. 6:13, 15, 18-20).

Marriage should be honored by all, and the marriage bed kept pure, for God will judge the adulterer and all the sexually immoral (Heb. 13:4).

ROOTS OF SEXUAL COMPULSION

Regina was the only daughter of a wealthy Italian family. A happy child, she was dearly loved and brought up in the church. She was still childlike at thirteen, but early development had given her the appearance of a woman. Vinnie saw her at church and was immediately attracted to her beauty.

Since Regina was not yet allowed to date, Vinnie visited her often and convinced her parents he was just the boy for Regina, even though he was a ripe old sixteen. His parents, wanting to encourage their son's relationship with a Christian girl, helped out by inviting Regina's folks for dinner.

Regina had never had a boyfriend before and was swept away by Vinnie's adoring attention. She was flattered that this handsome, debonair creature chose her out of all the girls at church. He was experienced, romantic, called all the shots, and she was anxious to please him. Regina was in love, and she believed it would last forever.

Vinnie took advantage of Regina's innocence. He had a car that made it easy for him to seduce her and teach her how to please him sexually. Their parents never suspected until much later, long after Vinnie had moved on to a new love. A series of loves, in fact.

Regina spent the rest of her life, literally, trying to get him back. In the process, she became sexually compulsive, trying to feel what she had first felt with him at thirteen. Or perhaps to reassure herself that although Vinnie had rejected her, she was still desirable. Known as a girl without shame, she was hardly selective in her promiscuity, as though frantically attempting to fill some urgent void.

Regina's parents couldn't get their daughter to talk, and they had no idea of her secret sins. Distant, depressed, and moody, she lacked interest in school and went through boyfriends in rapid succession. "Seems like she'll never find anyone she loves like Vinne," her mother often commented.

Regina was found dead at age twenty, an empty bottle of sleeping pills on the floor by her bed. A young man who had slept with her the night before recalled her mood as cheerful. Yet, after he left she made an entry in her diary. *Why wouldn't Vinnie love her?*

All do not react as severely as Regina, but many end up acting out their sexual confusion as she did. She became an addict, and her addiction took her life.

If this scenario is one with which you identify, I hope you have no lingering harmful effects. However, if you suspect some, ask yourself what beliefs and attitudes you formed out of your earliest sexual experiences. As an adult woman, you have grown in your emotional maturity. You can look at the past more objectively, and pick out the faulty conclusions once drawn by your youthful mind.

Even girls who insist they feel no guilt about sleeping around feel enormous self-doubt. A woman who lives that way cannot keep her self-esteem intact. As she moves from partner to partner, she begins to wonder if she is only an object. Some girls subconsciously hate men and try to view themselves as "the users." This is their way to continue their driven lifestyle while denying the sense of helplessness and powerlessness they actually feel.

Other experiences can also lead to compulsive behavior, especially abuse, rape, and incest. One in three women growing up in our country today is molested. I hate that statistic; I want to change it and make at least my own community a safe place for our girls to live. Those who have been molested cannot be forgotten; they need help and healing. Many of them, through no fault of their own, develop distortions in their sexuality.

Two specific examples come to mind. Both were unsuspecting teenage girls and told a tragic story of gang rape. Both were severely, irrevocably damaged by the experience; one became a compulsive eater, growing extremely fat, and the other developed a reputation for loose living, becoming mindlessly compulsive about sex. "I felt so dirty and worthless after the rape," Connie said, "like I needed to punish myself for being such a slut that those guys could do such horrible things to me."

In actuality, "those guys" were the criminals, not Connie. She had simply happened to walk by after they discussed rape over their beers. One dared the others to do what they'd just bragged about. Connie was not "chosen" because she was a bad person. She was a thirteen-year-old victim of evil.

Connie's fear of those brutal men kept her silent for years. They'd threatened to kill her parents if she told. Since she couldn't talk, she couldn't receive help, and her delusion about her own worthlessness grew. She began to act like the worthless girl she believed herself to be. As well as proving it to herself, now she had others, including her parents, believing the delusion: Connie is a worthless, vile, rotten girl.

As horrifying as the rape was, all by itself, Connie's experiences in subsequent years compounded her pain. A long chain of "love affairs" with men who mistreated her. A growing confusion about sex: "What's it for, anyway?" Some women respond to rape with a general phobia of all men. Connie went the other way, as though determined to keep trying until she got it right! She could have avoided so much pain if. . . .

If what? If she had immediately told her parents. If her parents had called the police. If the police had arrested the men and faced them with justice. She could have received the counseling so essential to restoring her mental equilibrium and positive feelings about herself. She could have come to understand that these men had committed an unfair, unjust crime against her. Not because she deserved it. Not because she was worthless.

Even in such tragic events as rape and abuse we hear simplistic solutions such as "A Christian woman should forgive and forget." Actually, other matters come first. Christian forgiveness does not excuse rapists, enabling them to run wild on our streets. It does not justify leaving a rape victim alone with her pain and nightmares.

Forgiveness is not to pretend that you were not harmed when your stepfather molested you, nor is it to ignore the ongoing effects of incest in your family. These diseases are cyclic if untreated. Each generation repeats the abuse of its parents. Christians should be the first to put a stop to the cycle; the first to demand treatment for the abuser and insist on compassionate help for the victim.

Victims of rape, abuse, incest, or other sexual traumas need emergency treatment. If my child lay bleeding on the highway, I would immediately take her to the nearest hospital. You would be horrified if I were to say, "Just forgive that driver who hit you, dear. Let's forget about it and go on with our lives!"

Because many trauma victims have not received treatment—not even a Band-aid—countless women in our midst are walking wounded. Some of them, quite understandably, were left feeling very mixed-up about sex.

INCEST

Some sexual addictions have their roots in the family. A cause and effect relationship may exist between incest and compulsive behavior. A large portion of women who suffer from alcoholism and eating disorders were abused as children or teenagers.

The trauma of childhood abuse is most severe and long-lasting when the abuse comes from a parent. What greater victimization can a child endure? Is escape possible when the people you depend on for survival cannot be trusted?

When medical science developed ways of measuring stress, it was found that people who suffered parental abuse grew up in the highest possible degree of stress. Theirs was worse by far than that of children who lived through the World War II air raids, shivering in London bomb shelters.

If you are an undeserving victim, the effects of your suffering will not go away by themselves. Blocking it out of your mind is not the answer; trying to forget and forgive will not work. God heals, but your part is to cooperate with him.

If you have never dealt with this part of your past, then you have work to do *before* you attempt forgiveness. Don't use easy forgiveness as a cloak. You should suspect a forgiveness that is too glib, even if it's couched in religious-sounding language. There is a place for forgiveness in your healing journey, but don't use it to avoid facing what happened to you and how it has influenced your attitudes and beliefs.

In their book on this subject, Pamela Vredevelt and Kathy Rodriguez describe how a girl is affected in her later years:

Seductive fathers condition their daughters to believe they can only get attention if they behave in a sexual way. These women highly emphasize their physical appearance, since Dad rewarded it, but they also experience conflicting feelings. They hated their fathers' advances, yet sexual attention was better than no attention at all. Consequently, their future relationships often have a strong sexual element before true intimacy develops.

Since, as children, (incest) victims have not been nurtured or had healthy experiences of male love, they are vulnerable to any kind of male attention, even the wrong kind. In their quest for nurturance, they often get into relationships that revictimize and abuse them. Research has shown that a victim's style of expression usually centers on her need for attention and love.[1]

If your father sexually abused you, no matter his reasons, he was wrong. Even if he quoted scripture to justify his actions. Even if he said, "I love you" along with his incest.

FACING THE TRUTH

Jesus reminded us that the truth will set us free. A look at the naked truth may cause pain, but it is the doorway into freedom. Perhaps you couldn't trust your parents, but you can trust God. He will not desert you or leave you hurting. He will reveal the truth. The more you see the truth, the more he can correct the distortions your child's mind developed around those events that were so frightening. He will not take you faster than you are capable of going, and he will embrace and comfort you all the way through. You'll emerge into a happier, wider world. Your vision will clear and your spirit free from the binding fears and compulsions that control you. This healing needs the guidance of a trained professional. Not just anyone, no matter how well-intentioned, is able to help.

A CHRISTIAN SEX OFFENDER?

"He claims he's a Christian. But a Christian would never molest his daughter, would he? How can someone who claims to be a believer sexually abuse a child?" The words *Christian* and *sex offender* seem like opposites. However, research shows that sexual abuse does take place within Christian circles.

Offenders distort reality with fragmented thinking. They may attend church on Sunday, molest on Monday and Tuesday, and be back in church on Wednesday. By compartmentalizing and neatly separating spirituality from their home life, they manage to maintain a fictional life of upstanding fatherhood.

Some incest victims say their fathers were deacons in church and highly respected members of the community. However, children like Janet saw a different side of Dad:

While I was growing up, my dad insisted we all attend church each Sunday. He beamed with pride, showing off his family. It all seemed extremely hypo-critical to me. Dad acted holy on Sunday, but before the week was over took advantage of me and my sister. Everyone in our town thought he was a perfect Christian father.

I never talked to people about what Dad was really like. They wouldn't have believed me anyway. Why should they? Dad looked as if he had it all together. I was just a scrawny little kid who jumped if anyone said, "Boo!" My insides churned when people bragged about him. It was even worse when Mom believed them. Only my sister and I knew the truth. I wish I had been courageous enough to expose him. Perhaps my life wouldn't be as topsy-turvy today, if I had gone to the authorities.[2]

Sex offenders are unaware of their own inconsistencies. They split spiritual life and behavior into two mutually exclusive domains. A Christian counselor wrote about Tim, a sex offender, who

tried to convince me he was unique ... because he was a believer: Tim said, "Because they aren't Christians, the people from Children's Protective Services don't understand me. I've asked God to heal me and firmly believe He has answered my prayer. But that stupid agency treats me like every other molester in town. They're making me live away from home and are even talking about a jail sentence. They don't understand that God has already freed me from this sin. There's nothing to worry about now. I've been healed."

Offenders such as Tim minimize the seriousness of their sexual behavior in light of their profession of faith. While denying the reality of his offensive behavior, Tim tried to convince me of his "uniqueness." He had no empathy for the pain and humiliation he had inflicted upon his daughters. Skirting the consequences was his sole concern.

Somehow Tim felt that his membership in God's family exempted him from the natural consequences of his actions. He said he was not like every other molester in town and indignantly objected to being treated as a common child abuser. However, God requires Tim to take his behavior very seriously and to highly regard the effects of his ungodly actions. The Lord never looks lightly at sin, especially when innocent victims can become further exploited if the sin isn't handled.[3]

Whether or not the person who abused you gets help, as a victim, you still need to seek help for yourself. That should be a serious priority in your life; *don't put it off!*

When a victim has developed her own sexual problem, what should she do? Start with the immediate problem—the addiction. In treatment, the causes will surface, but admitting the problem is the first step. It may also be your biggest obstacle. Denial and rationalization are deeply imbedded in addiction. Some common myths and rationalizations addicts tell themselves, according to specialist Patrick Carnes:

"I am oversexed."

"No one else is like me."

"I really did care for him."

"Just one more time won't hurt."

"I deserve it."

"It isn't so bad since everyone does it."

"He wanted, deserved, asked for it."[4]

Dr. Carnes states that rationalization and denial lead to sincere delusion, that is, believing your own lies. The end result is a gradual progression into insanity. Impaired thinking takes over.

In recovering from such insanity, your thought processes and reasonings must be scrutinized and challenged. The Bible speaks of a cleansed mind, a renewed mind, a mind given to learning the truth and self-control. This passage is especially practical for a woman who struggles with addiction: "It is God's will that you should be sanctified; that you should avoid sexual immorality; that each of you should *learn to control his own body* in a way that is holy and honorable, not in passionate lust like the heathen, who do not know God" (1 Thes. 4:3-5 italics added).

When your life is totally at the mercy of sexual appetites, you are no longer a free person. You are not living the life of a "free spirit." You are not "sexually liberated." When physical passions drive you and dominate your choices, freedom is no longer yours; *you are a slave.*

If sexuality forces you to serve it, rather than your own best interests, it is sexuality gone awry. The Bible says sexual sin is a sin you commit *against yourself* (see 1 Cor. 6:18).

Guilt tears you apart because deep inside you know you are too valuable for such behavior. Guilt persists even if you convince yourself you are not harming anyone else. Rather than becoming a more whole, integrated person, you are fracturing yourself. You're torn in half with self-doubt, inner conflicts, and guilt. Sex is no longer your friend but your enemy. Not a very healthy way to live!

But this is not the end. Sexual expression should make you feel loved, worthwhile, and cherished. God has a better life for you, and learning to control physical appetites is part of it.

Many of the early Christians had this problem, but they found help: "At one time we too were foolish, disobedient, deceived and enslaved by all kinds of passions and pleasures . . . But when the kindness and love of God our Savior appeared, he saved us, not because of righteous things we had done, but because of his mercy" (Titus 3:3-5).

For many, the transformation is a process. When we find ourselves confused, struggling with internal conflicts, and wondering what to believe, it takes some extensive mental rearranging before our mind starts working right. God has some educating to do. What was available to those early believers still is today: "For the grace of God that brings salvation teaches us . . . to say '*no*' to ungodliness and worldly passions, and to live self-controlled, upright and godly lives" (Titus 2:11-12).

SEEKING HELP

If you are in bondage to sexual compulsions, you need to seek God's help as well as the help of professionals trained in these problems. By seeking God's help, I mean something more than a quick, "Please, God, forgive me. I'll never do it again." Also, I don't mean you should spend a month browbeating yourself and trying to feel miserable; doing penance by feeling bad. Making yourself feel like slime will not solve the problem.

Trying too hard to "never do it again," gritting your teeth, and making grand resolutions may actually work against you. So will self-punishment when you fail.

God wants to teach you a healthy and satisfying way to get your true needs met. One that will leave you more whole, not divided against yourself. As you relax in the wonderful grace of God, which is that incredible quality he has of embracing you when you don't deserve it, the teaching will come naturally sensibly and in ways you can understand.

The problem of sexual addiction is better understood and more treatable today than ever before. Using methods developed by Alcoholics Anonymous, including the twelve-step process, many sexually addicted persons are recovering.

Take charge of your life *today*. Take the first step toward relief and recovery by consulting with an experienced professional qualified to treat sexual addiction. This is as urgent as if you had just received a diagnosis of a severe cancer or liver disease. Act immediately before this affliction wrecks your life and the lives of others. With recovery and healing will come the ability to truly love and experience genuine fulfillment.

9
...

The Obsessed

Not far from our home, twenty-one-year-old Deidre was getting ready for school when her phone rang. It was Mark, the boyfriend she had broken up with the previous year. Mildly annoyed that he still wouldn't leave her alone, Deidre listened to his request. "Please, let me see you one last time. I know you don't want to get back together, but I need you to just talk to me. Please, Deidre!"

"OK, Mark, but this is the *last time*—promise?"

"Yeah. I promise I'll leave you alone if you see me one more time." She agreed to meet him at the park after her college classes that day.

It was the most serious mistake of her life. Mark was crazed with obsession. That afternoon, the police found two bodies, both shot through the head. By questioning people at the park that day, they pieced together the sequence of events. Mark was seen getting into Deidre's car where they sat and talked for about an hour. Then, suddenly pulling out a revolver, Mark killed her, saying goodbye to her for the last time as he'd promised. He then ran a short distance into the woods and shot himself.

Persons obsessed with a love object were once lightly dismissed as "hung up" or referred to as having trouble "getting over him." Certainly time would heal the hung-up victim, and he or she would find there were "other fish in the sea." Until some intense, dramatic movies and equally horrifying evening news dramas stimulated public awareness, we didn't believe obsession could lead to such tragic craziness.

Experts say it is much more common these days for "love" to make people crazy. Dangerous obsessions are on the rise. Fatal attractions will cause many more deaths and injuries than in past years. In a rational state of mind, we know that love doesn't shoot people. But the victim of obsession is not rational. He'll say, "It was because I loved her so much."

One man attacked a business, fired a gun at computers, and injured employees in order to take his former girlfriend hostage in her office. He was interviewed after being sent to prison for this crime.

"I loved Kathy so much. I just had to see her. I had to prove my love for her—show her that I'd stop at nothing to get even one hour with her. The risk was worth it. I felt so good when we were finally alone in her office."

Kathy was not impressed with this dramatic "proof" of love. Instead, she was terrified and still suffers nightmares and fears, anticipating the day her "lover" is released from prison. She feels she will never be safe until he's dead. In no way does she attribute his actions to love.

"He was normal when I first met him—at least I thought he was. I dated him some, but I didn't feel romantic toward him. When I told him I didn't intend to marry him or even date him exclusively, he started acting weird. It got worse and worse, and then finally he went berserk."

These two incidents happen to involve men as the obsessed persons. But men have no corner on the business. Remember Robin, in a previous chapter, who ended up a suicide victim as a result of her obsession with Sam?

That experience was my first alarming encounter with romantic obsession. I had failed to recognize the seriousness of Robin's state of mind toward Sam and missed the opportunity to direct her out of obsession into freedom. I did not want to make that mistake again.

Most importantly, I should have made it clear to Robin that God was *not* the cause of her persistent feelings of attachment to Sam.

"I've asked God to take away my love for Sam if we're not meant to be together," she said. "But the feelings don't leave. Guess God has a reason. He must want us to be together someday."

WRITING HER OWN NOVEL

The obsessed person lives in a fantasy world. Her fantasy distracts her as she mulls over scenes from the past, grasping from memory any comment she can add to her tokens of hope. She is busy writing her own romantic novel where love conquers all. The lady wins with her grand and noble devotion.

She is loyal to the man she's chosen no matter how he feels about her. He may be untrue to the fantasy, but she will never be. She will continue loving, giving, and hanging on to her hope no matter what obstacles are placed in front of her. He marries another woman. What is that compared to her noble faith and love? Merely a small interference, nothing permanent.

139

She is impressed with the grandeur and brilliance of her love. It has such a Christian, enduring quality, much like God's love for those who reject him. Besides, how can she, a Christian, a loving person, ever reject or hate a man she has once loved? When she falls in love, it is forever.

At church she hears a sermon about the unconditional, giving love of God, and she is cheered, buoyed up in her determination. The pastor reads from 1 Corinthians 13 that love is patient and is not proud. It is not selfish nor easily angered. Love always trusts, hopes, and perseveres. Love never fails. Her feelings match the description; her desires are for the best and noblest. This is nothing less than the love of God! He has given her a supernatural love!

Although the victim often glamorizes her obsession, she is exceedingly miserable. Writing about women suffering from obsession, Drs. Connell Cowan and Melvyn Kinder share these experiences:

Arlene, a 36-year-old set designer for TV variety shows, was miserable after she broke up with Hal, 25, an actor, ten weeks ago. Unable to sleep night after night, she lost fifteen pounds from her already slender frame. This normally attractive, stable, and vivacious woman was literally pining away for Hal, who dropped her without warning for a 22-year-old rock singer.

Thoughts of Hal not only dominated her waking hours but also tormented her dreams—jealous dreams of confronting Hal with his new girlfriend. What was certainly as painful as the loss of Hal's love was the humiliation she felt at not being able to rid herself of his memory. She awoke with thoughts and fantasies of what he was doing at that moment. She went to sleep with the same pictures racing through her mind.

The fact that Hal was a regular on a show at the same studio made it even more difficult for Arlene. She found herself compulsively checking his parking space, so she could know whether or not he was on the studio lot. At first, she casually asked mutual friends about him and his new girlfriend as if she no longer cared. More recently, the questions had taken on a nakedly desperate tone. It was very apparent to her friends that Arlene was not letting go. She wrote him letters which she never mailed. She made many late-night phone calls to his apartment, only to hang up when "she" answered.

The final humiliation came one night when she made one of her increasingly frequent drives past his building to see if his lights were on. The windows were dark that evening, so Arlene parked her car on a side street where she could watch the entrance to his building. She fell asleep and was awakened by a tapping on her window. To her horror, it was Hal. Arlene opened her eyes to see his amazed face and "her" not three feet away, sitting in Hal's parked car. Arlene watched, paralyzed, as Hal, shaking his head, turned away. He opened the door for the young woman and pointedly put his arm around her as they walked up the sidewalk.

Glenda, a 30-year-old interior designer, still cried herself to sleep more often than not eight months after her boyfriend Ward fumbled through his final good-byes. Theirs had been a heady, fast, and volatile relationship. They seemed to share so many interests, particularly their love of the outdoors. They had often gone backpacking and had spent many a glorious sunset together. She introduced Ward to the design world she loved so much. He got her interested in running.

Glenda felt close and content. But what seemed like near perfection started to crumble when Ward inexplicably began to pull away. Her strong need to understand and to hold him only served to speed his retreat. Before she could even begin dealing with the thought that she was losing Ward, she had lost him.

Glenda couldn't believe that she was alone and that he was really gone for good. She found herself having long dialogues with him in her head—some warm and nostalgic, others hurt and angry, still others raw and pleading. So silent and private was her grief, even her closest friends thought she was handling the situation like a champ. She wasn't.

Restaurants, songs, theaters, even outfits she re-membered wearing with him were nagging reminders of his absence. When she was alone, which was al-most all the time she wasn't at work, Glenda's thoughts turned to self-recrimination and ceaseless recapitulation of what she might have said or done differently, as if hitting upon that perfect explanation might somehow change things—might magically bring him back.

Glenda explained, "I know it's over and that he isn't coming back, but I just keep on thinking about him. I know it's ridiculous to hope, but I do anyway."

Jackie, a 28-year-old secretary, broke up with Al-len, a journalist, two years ago. Since that time, she has dated many men, but none compare, even come close to, Allen. Jackie believed he was the one "just right" man for her. Sophisticated and from a family of high achievers, he seemed to possess all the right qualities. She loved his family and adopted them as her own. Jackie also greatly enjoyed Allen's many and interesting friends, who ranged from struggling artists to political types.

Jackie felt a sense of completion in Allen's presence. She felt more womanly, sexier, and more whole than at any other time she could remember. In her most private and honest moments, however, Jackie had to admit that some of the sense of perfection in Allen was filled in by her hopeful, eager wishes. In truth, Allen was far from perfect.

Allen's one passion was his work.... When it came to relationships, they took a definite back seat. Jackie talked about her wishes to get married and have a family; Allen spoke with excitement about the possibility of a bureau chief assignment in Beirut. When Allen was offered and accepted the job overseas, Jackie's bright hopes turned to disappointment and despair.

Allen wrote twice a week for the first month or so, and Jackie answered each letter. Both were careful to sound casual. The letters became shorter, then fewer, then they stopped. Jackie forced herself to see other men, but she felt no one could match Allen or ignite the special feeling she had had when she was with him.

And Jackie was right. Every man she went out with, she compared to Allen. Every one came up short. Jackie soon realized she was looking to find Allen in them, and, of course, he wasn't there. Her dogged search made it impossible for her to see any of the unique qualities her dates did have. Other men didn't fully exist because they were not Allen.

Jackie, sadly, believes Allen is not simply one man she loved, but the "only" man for whom she could have those wonderful, dizzy feelings of love. "I still have fantasies that he will come back and we'll start where we left off. I know that thinking this way is probably not very realistic, but that's the way it is."

These women have one important thing in common. Each is endlessly mourning a lost love. And while the pain these women experience is terribly real and terribly sad, it is also self-defeating. The central difficulty in an extended mourning process is a search not so much for the perfect man, but for the perfect feeling of love.[1]

Counselors Cowan and Kinder believe:

Although the grieving process must be gone through, the prolongation of this process is related to the difficulty many women have in coming to grips with the issues of victimization and low self-esteem.

The problem of prolonged mourning plagues far more women than it does men. It's certainly not that men are rejected less frequently, or that they feel less pain. The difference lies in their solutions to the problem. Men tend to handle rejection, even from someone they loved deeply, by reconnecting with another woman, often surprisingly quickly. Many women inadvertently attempt to deal with the wound of rejection through continued fantasies about getting back together with the man who rejected them—a self-defeating and painful choice. . . . Because connectedness is so central for women, they will take chances and put forth heroic efforts to salvage or restore a relationship.[2]

DON'T CALL IT UNCONDITIONAL LOVE!

To kid yourself into believing your obsession is Christian or unconditional love is a colossal mistake. Love respects another's choices. Love does not possess nor ignore the rights of another.

Genuine love may have motivated your feelings at one time, but when demand took over, love ceased. Your need became pre-eminent and meeting that need the major goal. Vast difference exists, pointed out Erich Fromm, between "infantile love" and "mature love." Immature love says, "I love you because I need you." Mature love says," I need you because I love you."

Of course, this distinction is hard to make when you are in the throes of obsession. Need and love blur. The obsession, like a drug addiction, has its own voice and reasoning. It has its own unreal world that unfortunately *is* real to the obsessed person.

HE KEEPS ME FROM WORSHIP

A pastor confronted 34-year-old Clint about Louanne's complaints. She loved her church, but felt she couldn't attend services anymore because of his behavior toward her. Clint insisted Louanne meet with the pastor and him to discuss their problems. Reluctantly, she agreed.

The pastor began, "Clint says he loves you and believes you love him, Louanne. I'd like to know how you feel. He says you don't want to go out with him anymore and won't even talk to him about it."

"I've talked till I'm blue in the face. There's nothing more to say. We dated a little, but I never felt romantic about Clint. He can't seem to believe that. I'm sorry, Clint, I don't want to hurt your feelings, but I've been trying nicely to ease out of this, and you need to believe me.

Please don't keep calling and writing letters.

"Pastor," she said, "it's so embarrassing. I never know when he's going to make a scene at church. I can't relax and enjoy a service anymore; I'm always on edge wondering what he's going to pull next!"

The pastor looked closely at Clint. Perhaps now he would give up his bizarre stunts, having heard from Louanne's own lips that she did not love him and never had felt the way he presumed she had. "Clint, you've heard what she wants. How about respecting her wishes and calling a halt to all this? Leave her alone, and go on with your life."

Clint was stolid. His eyes revealed that her words hadn't reached him. "Whatever she says now," he replied, "doesn't matter. I know how it's all going to turn out. I'm not discouraged. I'll always love her."

Louanne looked upset and fearful as he continued. His voice took a deep, resonant tone of spiritual conviction: "God spoke to me. He pointed Louanne out during a service and said, '*She is your wife.*' This is his fault, not mine!"

Despite the efforts of friends to help him, Clint remained delusioned. He phoned Louanne, showed up at her work, sent flowers—all this even after she refused to respond, lest she encourage his hopes. Then he became deeply depressed and unable to sleep. He lost weight and couldn't concentrate on his work. But he still believed Louanne would change her mind. He was sure God gave him the drive and ability to feel with such intensity so that he would not give up. He would persevere and do God's will in spite of all obstacles; Louanne, the pastor, church, friends, even his job and his health. God had created this woman especially for him.

A TENACIOUS DELUSION

Clint's experience illustrates the tenacious nature of obsession and how it can withstand even the most blatant truth. If you happen to be in Louanne's position, don't be fooled into cooperating with the delusion.

Make a clean break and stick to it. Refuse to respond to the obsessed person in any way—even negatively. If you are in physical danger, call the police immediately. Do not feed the obsession with a smile or anything that might keep the flame of hope alive.

QUESTION THE "VOICE"

If, on the other hand, you are the victim of an obsession in which you believe, like Clint, that you have heard from God, it is time to question the voice. Our desperate emotional needs can fool us into imagining that God is saying something we earnestly desire to hear. God wants you to have a fulfilling life. If a marriage partner is part of that life, he had better be someone who has freely chosen you and who deeply desires to spend his life with you.

God does not force anyone into marriage. Isn't it obvious that Clint would not find happiness married to Louanne? Neither would you find real joy in a marriage you manipulated into existence. Deep inside, you want a marriage in which you are totally loved and chosen for yourself alone. It's only possible as you give up your obsession and recognize it for what it is.

As a victim of obsession, you feel powerless at the mercy of another person's choices. This helplessness brings on depression and panic. It exists because you have given someone else too much power. You have allowed another person control of your identity or value. No one has the right to control those parts of you.

Take back the power you gave away! Make choices independently of what "he" might think. Stop ordering your life around seeing him or talking on the phone with him.

Take charge of your life, and make choices that will build up your sagging self-worth; choices that nurture good relationships with friends and family, choices that allow the development of your talents and skills, choices which allow you to feel the pleasure of accomplishment and creativity. Consider going to college or taking some classes. Cultivate new friendships. Shake yourself awake and relish the joys you've missed while centered on him.

HELP IS URGENT!

Obsession is the most dangerous of the counterfeits discussed in this book. Obsession can go on for years, enslaving its victim and jeopardizing the safety of others. Because of its addictive and deceptive nature, you can't beat it alone. Set up an appointment with a counseling center to get professional treatment. One conversation with a sympathetic pastor or friend is *not enough*. Don't do that and then say, "I tried counseling and it didn't help. I still feel the same."

That conclusion is premature. Obsession is far too stubborn to give way as the result of one tentative conversation. Like other addictions, obsession is sustained by powerful habits of denial and impaired thinking.

INTENSE EMOTIONAL NEEDS

Your personal and emotional needs are great. Your focus on the other person intensifies those feelings and blocks all other avenues to meeting your needs.

In your awareness of pain and longing, you crave immediate relief. You believe you can find that relief in the arms of the one you desire. But God has a better, a long-term answer. An answer you grow into. God can use even this troubling time to bring about many good and transforming changes in you. In those inner changes lies the answer to these desperate needs. Immediate relief is only a substitute for the personal growth that will bring ultimate fulfillment of those longings.

But Band-aid relief only camouflages the seriousness of the problem and postpones your long-term cure. Stuck in endless mourning, you miss life—perhaps years of it.

FEAR OF GRIEF

Sometimes obsession grows out of a fear of facing grief. "I can't let go of the hope I'll get him back," said Courtney. "It would be too painful to live without hope. I know I could never stand it."

Fear of grief is not an irrational fear. Grief is real and our normal emotional response to loss. We risk it each time we allow ourselves to love someone. Appropriate grieving is different than endless mourning. It includes healing, too.

Clinging to your obsession may be a last-ditch attempt to escape the process of grief. You know you're kidding yourself; it really is over, but you can't yet accept the fact.

STAGES OF GRIEF

An early stage of grief is denial: "This isn't really happening. There must be some mistake."

Then comes bargaining: "Please, God, I'll go to church every Sunday if you'll give him back to me. I'll be a missionary. I'll never sin again."

Bargaining gives way to anger. We feel the loss and it hurts.

Next comes depression. As these stages progress, we

gradually accept the loss and are eventually able to move into the future. "*Blessed* are those who mourn, for they will be comforted," said Jesus (Matt. 5:4 italics added). The grief process is God's provision for our healing when we suffer loss. He sticks close to the one who mourns and gives comfort through the journey from loss to acceptance.

As a Christian, you will never suffer grief alone. God's comfort and embrace will be real to you once you acknowledge the loss and mourn it. Other believers will support you, too, if you give them a chance, and let them know what you're walking through. Seek out their support, and let them pray for you and with you. Let them love you; don't try to be the Lone Ranger. God's desire is "to comfort all who mourn, and provide for those who grieve in Zion—to bestow on them a crown of beauty instead of ashes, the oil of gladness instead of mourning, and a garment of praise instead of a spirit of despair" (Isa. 61:2,3).

The end of grief is not despair, despondency, hopelessness, and endless sadness. Grief's end is better than its beginning. And it is immeasurably better than the tortured state of obsession.

10

• • •

The Darling

A cute little girl, the Darling was always cuddled, held, and told she was lovable. She somehow forgot to grow beyond the childish delight of being the Darling. As an adult, she continues to be coy, childlike, and cute. She is most comfortable when others hold, soothe, and take care of her.

I discovered this tendency as I was preparing an earlier book, *Ordinary Women—Extraordinary Strength*. Wherever I happened to be speaking, I asked women, "Why are we afraid of our strength?" In nearly every location, at least one person replied, "Because it's easier to be weak and be taken care of." Invariably, a rippling of knowing laughter filled the room.

"If we admit our strength, they'll expect a lot more of us," added another woman. "We'll have to take on more responsibility."

Playing the lovable little girl, dependent and needy, seems to work for some women. They find scriptural encouragement, they believe, in verses they quote about submission to husbands and "leadership in the home."

NO DECISIONS

One husband complained to me that his wife wouldn't choose new carpeting for the family room, insisting, "You're the decision-maker, dear."

Some women have tried playing "darling little girl" because they believe it is what God wants. Their childish behavior is proposed as "Christian" by some writers of books on marriage and speakers in churches and marriage seminars. One such speaker addressed a women's group in our congregation. He emphasized the differences between men and women, and said, "Women can remain little girls while men must grow up. We don't give boys permission to remain childish; they are anxious to grow up and be men; it's their nature. But women are more lovable when they are cute, girlish, and young; it's more feminine. We men like women who stay like little girls."

NOT MADE FOR RESPONSIBILITY

Many women voiced to me their difficulty receiving this speaker's opinions on the distinctives of men and women. But he was not alone in expressing, in the name of God, the belief that women were never intended to assume responsibility for their own lives, let alone any other important responsibilities.

Elizabeth Rice Handford wrote that a woman is never given the right to live her life independent of a man's "authority." She is cared for by her father until marriage, and after marriage she is responsible to her husband, to obey him as God's divinely appointed guardian and master.

While she recognizes that it may be hard, especially when the husband is cruel, godless, or commands her to do things that go against her conscience, Mrs. Rice points out this advantage: *"You Have Freedom From the Consequence of Decisions.* When you give back to your husband the responsibility for the direction of the home and the making of decisions, you also give him the responsibility for the consequences of his decisions."[1]

She quotes a woman who said it made life much simpler to turn over all choices to her husband. "Now he makes the decisions, and he's stuck with them!"[2]

WOMEN DON'T HAVE CONFIDENCE

"Fortunately, that's the way a man likes it. God made a man to be aggressive, to respond to challenge, to glory in his manhood, to rejoice in draining his strength, to risk great hazards for the one he loves. . . . a woman . . . doesn't have confidence in her physical strength, in her ability to cope with danger, in her decision-making ability. It is a privilege, a gift unearned, for a woman to have a man take upon himself her welfare."[3]

This same writer insists that God will protect the woman who obeys even when her guardian commands her to commit sin. Her part is to unconditionally trust the man who has authority over her, and all will be well. Unfortunately, this has not been the case for the thousands of Christian women who struggle with abuse from their supposed guardians. Beaten, bruised, but afraid to leave the house to seek help, they silently endure suffering because they believe they are helpless little girls, unable to survive without a man to father them, even a man who beats and punishes, kicks and demeans.

TREMBLE AND QUIVER

Not too many years ago, countless women were influenced by *Fascinating Womanhood,* a book and "marriage course" that delineated specific ways to win the devotion of a man by emphasizing little girl qualities and childlike behaviors. Men are amused, said the writer, when their women pout, tremble, quiver, stamp their feet, or let tears trickle down their cheeks. If a man says something unkind, a woman can swish out the door, slam it hard, and say, "You big meany!" or "I'll tell your mother on you!"

HIDE YOUR CAPABILITIES

Women are taught that "feminine dependency" should be exaggerated so that men can feel masculine. For example, never demonstrate capability in the presence of a man, especially when performing a "masculine task." (Something a woman should never be asked to do in the first place, i.e. fixing the faucet, mowing the lawn, etc.)[4]

In newer editions of *Fascinating Womanhood,* the author has modified some of her suggestions for emphasizing little girl appeal. Her intentions were to save marriages by helping wives win the love of their husbands. However, this kind of advice leads women to put a stop to their growth and deny their capabilities for fear of becoming unattractive to men.

UNFAIR TO MEN?

In such thought systems, men are pictured with precarious egos; their masculinity lost in the mere presence of an adult woman. Writers with these beliefs quote Bible verses about women submitting to men and leave out verses that include men in submission. They claim men have a superior role that women need to bolster with girlish trust, dependency, reverence, and unquestioning obedience.

UNFAIR USE OF SCRIPTURE

Such use of scripture may be convincing but it can also discourage women from taking responsibility for themselves and growing into mature adults.

A faulty, one-sided definition of submission causes women to accept a self-concept in which they are inferior to all men. They live out this image of themselves until it becomes a habit to throw all decisions on men, blame men for everything wrong in their lives, and harbor resentment toward husbands for failing to meet all their needs.

As we pointed out in the chapter about the Matriarch, it is always important to remember the clear instructions of Jesus about relationships of control and domination. These are forbidden to Christian believers, male or female. Philippians 2:1-8 describes a healthy love relationship where mutual respect rules out any desire to control or use another person.

It takes a shallow and warped knowledge of scripture to actually believe God wants women to remain little girls all their lives. You must close your eyes to all the passages that admonish growth in maturity, all the verses exhorting us to walk in the strength, might, and power of Christ. And those that tell us to put away childishness, manipulation, deceit, and trickiness.

The Bible is full of capable, strong, responsible women, and we are told to follow their example, not abhor it in fear of losing our childishness. Not once in the Bible are women told to pretend they are something they are not, or to put on an act of weakness, fearfulness, or stupidity.

DARLING DAUGHTERS

Jerry and I have two daughters, Carmen and Christi.

When they were toddlers, we often referred to them as Princess Number One and Princess Number Two. Later, we sometimes called each one Darling Daughter—and still today you might overhear us affectionately use the term.

I remember a day during my early motherhood when the girls were especially enjoyable and loving. An amazing insight flashed into my mind: *they are the perfect ages!* Carmen was five and Christi three. They were the cutest, sweetest, most wonderful children in the universe. Each was delightful as a bouncing baby, but somehow, I thought, *They are more fun now than ever before.* This discovery of the "perfect age," of course, was followed by the statement heard from mothers everywhere: "If I could just keep them these ages."

My attitude extended to friends whose children were a little older. Six- and eight-year-old girls looked rather boring to me; they were tall and gangly. They had spaces in their smiles where teeth used to be. I felt a small tinge of pity for mothers whose darling daughters had passed the perfect ages.

ANOTHER INSIGHT

Fortunately for my daughters, I soon forgot my insight about the perfect ages. We did the same things most parents do for kids; fed them, gave them educational toys, sent them to school, taught them how to manage money, drive a car, and launder their clothes. Of course, these actions are not consistent with the desire to keep children five and three years old. So a day arrived when we experienced another amazing insight: both Darling Daughters had grown up!

Today, Carmen and Christi are capable, adult women. Aside from Jerry, they are my two best friends—there is not even a close competitor. They are no longer the perfect ages of five and three. They have grown (and are growing) far beyond anything the mother of those little girls could have imagined. They are my equals; they are strong, creative, and loving women who inspire me. I love watching Carmen care for her children and seeing Christi manage all the business details of her office. I can laugh at my immature desire to keep them stuck as little girls. What a tragedy it would be if we mothers were granted that wish!

BASED ON IGNORANCE

The impulse to keep them little was based not only on the joy of early mothering, but also on ignorance. Since I had not experienced the pleasures of adult daughters, I didn't understand what I would miss if they failed to grow up.

Something similar takes place in the attitudes of the Darling. Adulthood has never been experienced; it's an unknown. Childhood is more fun, safer, and less stress-filled. Like Peter Pan, we can easily make small choices that add up to an "I don't want to grow up" decision. It may be a decision based on the pleasures and positives of childhood. Or an attitude born out of the unhappiness modeled by our parents. Either way, we choose out of ignorance. Until we experience the full force of adulthood with its pleasures as well as its responsibilities, we cannot know what we are depriving ourselves of.

Does this sound too stern? As if we ought to turn our backs on all the childlike qualities we possess and turn into grim matrons? Not at all! Keep all the good things— laughter, play, curiosity, readiness to learn, wonder, and affection. But add to those the characteristics of an adult.

ABIGAIL: BEAUTIFUL AND WISE

Read Abigail's story in 1 Samuel, and then try to imagine her response to the idea of putting on a little girl pout!

Abigail is a woman the Bible names as both intelligent and beautiful. God commended her for her wisdom and strength. Nor did her courage and capability turn off men. King David was so impressed he asked her to marry him.

Abigail was married to a rich rancher named Nabal. He was a bad-tempered, hardhearted, unpredictable guy. Near them, David and his men camped in the wilderness. David had recently been anointed king and would soon rule Israel. However, at this time, he and his band were hungry and running out of food.

David sent ten men to visit Nabal and told them:

> Say to him: "Long life to you! Good health to you and your household! And good health to all that is yours! Now I hear that it is sheep-shearing time. [This was a holiday season, a time for feasting, sharing and celebrating.] When your shepherds were with us, we did not mistreat them, and the whole time they were at Carmel nothing of theirs was missing. Ask your own servants and they will tell you. Therefore be favorable toward my young men, since we come at a festive time. Please give your servants and your son David whatever you can find for them" (1 Sam. 25:5-8).

The young soldiers delivered the request but received quite a surprise from Nabal. Loudly playing the fool, he pretended he'd never heard of David. Why should he share his food with a bunch of "men from who knows where?" Ignoring the servants' reports of David's kindness, Nabal put on a front of pompous self-importance and arrogant power.

David must have had a short fuse that day because his response to his soldiers' foodless return was "Put on your swords! This fellow paid me back evil for good. By morning there won't be one male left alive in his entire household!" Off he went with four hundred soldiers, hungry, enraged, and armed.

Meanwhile, back at the ranch, one of the servants told Abigail: "David sent messengers from the desert to give our master his greetings, but he hurled insults at them. Yet these men were very good to us ... Night and day they were a wall around us all the time ... Now think it over and see what you can do, because disaster is hanging over our master and his whole household. He is such a wicked man that no one can talk with him" (1 Sam. 25:14-17).

A DECISIVE WOMAN

Abigail was decisive. She lost no time taking action. She gathered a little picnic for those hungry soldiers: two hundred loaves of bread, two skins of wine, five sheep ready for barbecue, a bushel of grain, plus plenty of their favorite desserts—raisin and fig cakes. She loaded all this on donkeys. "Then she told her servants, 'Go on ahead; I'll follow you.' But she did not tell her husband Nabal" (1 Sam. 25:19).

As she rode her donkey into a mountain ravine, David and his men descended toward her. When Abigail saw David, she quickly got off her donkey and bowed down before him with her face to the ground. She fell at his feet and took full responsibility: "My lord, let the blame be on me alone. Please let your servant speak to you; hear what your servant has to say. May my lord pay no attention to that wicked man Nabal. He is just like his name—his name is Fool, and folly goes with him. But as for me, your servant, I did not see the men my master sent" (1 Sam. 25:24,25).

She captured David's attention long enough to calm him down. He listened and she gave a brilliant speech. When she finished, David announced that God must have sent Abigail to meet him: "May you be blessed for your good judgement and for keeping me from bloodshed this day and from avenging myself with my own hands. Go home in peace. I have heard your words and granted your request" (1 Sam. 25:32,35).

Relieved, she returned home to find Nabal holding a "banquet like that of a king." He was drunk so Abigail didn't bother to tell him of his narrow escape. When Nabal sobered up, she told him "all these things, and his heart failed him and he became like a stone." Within two weeks Nabal was dead. David heard of his death and promptly sent servants to visit Abigail with a marriage proposal. As the story ends, "Abigail quickly got on a donkey and, attended by her five maids, went with David's messengers and became his wife" (1 Sam. 25:42).

Abigail was a spunky lady and a much more godly pattern for us adult women than our cute little girls. Genuine loving is an adult matter. Playing the role of a child will short circuit our attempts to live a life of Christian love. Abigail cared enough for her family and employees to readily take responsibility and protect them from danger. Love does not avoid responsibility by hiding behind a mask of feminine frailty or leaving all decisive action to men.

A DOTING FATHER

Some women are inadvertently taught the Darling role by their parents. Drs. Cowan and Kinder describe instances of this in a variety of family patterns:

Lynn was the only girl, the baby of the family, and the darling of her father's eye. Both parents focused their attention and adoration on Lynn, whose accomplishments were to go beyond anything the parents hoped to achieve personally. Her father was particularly dot-ing, giving her the material things he thought befitting his "little Princess." Lynn's bedroom was decorated and furnished far beyond the means of the parents and in sharp contrast to the rest of the apartment. Her father saw to it that she bought her clothes at only the finest stores. He even drove her across town each Sunday so she could attend church in a wealthier suburb. The more he gave, the more she wanted and the more she got. It's no wonder that "little Lynnie" grew into a voracious adult.

Initially warm and adoring with men, Lynn quickly became demanding and critical of anything less than the Herculean effort put forth by her father. She was absolutely determined to find a man who would also think, "There's nothing too good for my baby."

Lynn didn't hope men would give and do for her, she expected them to, without reservation, and with-out any realistic consideration on her part of the man's individual circumstances.

Finally, when Walt, a kind and very traditional man, proposed to her with proper ceremony and a sizable diamond ring, Lynn gave him a qualified yes. Lynn did get married, but she has never received the fuss and adoration she was led to believe she deserved. Her husband's resentment only increased as her demands mounted. Lynn's unrealistic expectations have led to chronic disappointment for her, and for Walt, a nag-ging feeling of inadequacy.[5]

Like Lynn, some women whose fathers doted on them learned a harmful pattern for relating to men. However, "The healthy, caring father is concerned about his daugh-ter's view of men. He doesn't allow his own needs for control and/or adoration to overly influence his behavior toward his daughter. He wants her to grow up as strong and capable as possible."[6]

THE POWERFUL FATHER

While a doting father may have brought about the Darling's self-absorbed definition of love, a powerful father is often over-idealized by his daughter. He is highly successful, competent, well-known, or authoritative. When she grows up, young men seem inadequate and weak in comparison to Dad. She doesn't realize her father took years to become the mature success she sees. She has a hard time accepting and loving a man her own age.

Often it is hard for women to break away from powerful fathers. A woman doesn't free herself from her father's physical presence. Going away to school or getting an apartment or a job does not necessarily change a woman's wish to be taken care of. That need is simply transferred to the "new man" in her life.

Breaking free of that dependent tie requires confronting and overcoming fears of independence, working through the anxiety that inevitably accompanies the process of becoming independent. It also requires a more realistic acceptance of men as they are, not as childhood fantasies would like them to be.

Women who have had an incomplete relationship with their fathers or no relationship at all have been deprived of normal experiences. What effect does not having had the experience of a father's love have upon the way these women view men as adults? When a girl lacks a father in her life, she creates a fantasy father. The fantasy is constructed from watching TV and movies, reading books, and observing other children's fathers. Bit by bit, a composite father takes form. The image that emerges is composed of the most interesting, comforting, and loving of elements. The fantasized, wished-for father is invariably strong and protective.

Such wishful dreaming is healthy in that the girl is nourished, to some degree, by the vision of what a good father could be. But there are often distortions. Rarely is there any acknowledgment of possible flaws.

The powerful longing for the father and his love often leads a woman to continue the search into adulthood. Anita, who at 34 has sadly not yet been able to sustain a happy, lasting relationship with a man, revealed, "My father died when I was two but I always had an idea of exactly what he was like. I dreamed about him as I got older. He would come in and help me or save me from something bad. I knew that if only he were around, I'd feel safe."

Anita's fantasy about her father has caused real interferences with men. She hasn't yet found anyone with whom she feels "safe," whom she can trust not to abandon her as her father did. In addition, the men she has been with haven't lived up to the image she constructed so long ago of what a man should be.[7]

Whatever our relationships with fathers, we can't blame them for our failure to grow up. Becoming an adult is ultimately our choice. Actually, it is a series of choices in which we assume responsibility for ourselves and give up more and more of our dependency on parents or parent substitutes. This is impossible for women who have confused little girl dependency with spirituality.

PARTNERSHIP

I willingly gave my independence up to become the life partner of a wonderful man; a small sacrifice in proportion to the benefits of married life. We did not want to live apart from each other. We joined our goals, desires, dreams, talents, strengths, weaknesses, failures, successes, hopes, fears.

Not everyone wants to do that. But we don't regret it. We chose to become interdependent rather than independent. A relationship between two interdependent adults is vastly different than one between two independent beings, both committed only to doing their own thing.

INTERDEPENDENCE

Once we chose to become life partners, we bought into the other's experiences, for better or worse. Interdependent people help each other out. They cry together, laugh together, give each other a listening ear when needed, or maybe a kick in the pants.

As trust grows in our relationships, we learn to depend on each other. This is healthy, pleasant, and normal. The Bible suggests it is the proper attitude for Christians to have toward each other. The church is a living organism made up of interdependent members:

Now the body is not made up of one part but of many. If the foot should say, "Because I am not a hand, I do not belong to the body," it would not for that reason cease to be part of the body. And if the ear should say, "Because I am not an eye, I do not belong to the body," it would not for that reason cease to be part of the body. If the whole body were an eye, where would the sense of hearing be? ... If they were all one part, where would the body be? As it is, there are many parts, but one body. The eye cannot say to the hand, "I don't need you!" And the head cannot say to the feet, "I don't need you!" (1 Cor. 12:14-17, 19-21).

For a mature adult, neither dependency or independence is necessary in a relationship. There is a third alternative: interdependence.

MOVE AWAY FROM DEPENDENCY

Perhaps you tend toward unhealthy, clinging dependency. A desperate, please-don't-leave-me-I'll-do-anything-if-you'll-just-love-me attitude. A move in the direction of independence would probably be good for you. Rather than end up a belligerent, lonely, self-sufficient porcupine, you'll become more capable of holding up your end of a responsible relationship.

Sometimes dependence is appropriate and a necessary prerequisite to interdependent living as I've described it. For example, we were dependent on our parents for many years, and rightly so.

Dependency is necessary when you are incapacitated. You may need skilled medical attention or round-the-clock nursing care in a hospital. How foolish to say at such a time, "I'm an independent woman. I can handle this myself!"

The goal of the hospital staff, of course, is to get you back on your feet. But for awhile, in order to regain your health, you must face dependency.

If you are dealing with an addiction, you have a problem that is destroying you physically as well as spiritually and mentally. People who try to achieve healing of their addictions on their own seldom succeed.

If you have a stubborn streak or pride yourself on your strong, independent nature, you will find it difficult to admit: "I need help." Even that confession, simple as it is, puts you in a dependent condition. You must allow others to help, and that feels uncomfortable.

I admire courageous women who have come to that point, women like Betty Ford and Kitty Dukakis, who had so much at stake, at least in the public eye. Having gained respect as capable and strong, they risked their image and became dependent, not only on clinic personnel, counselors, and nurses, but on their own families.

So, dependence at times is good, right and extremely necessary if you are to become the healthy, giving person you desire to be.

A TIME FOR INDEPENDENCE

Independence has its seasons also. As a mother, I have watched three, almost four children reach the point where independence is their goal. Possibly even their major value. That urge causes parents great concern, but isn't it a symptom of vibrant aliveness? We want our children to establish their own homes, pay their own bills, and relate to us as adults. Their independence from us feels like our success; we worked at least eighteen years to accomplish it.

When grown-up children mature to where they can give up their hard-earned independence and join with another adult in a loving partnership, our joy is doubled. Now they are committed to the challenges and pleasures of interdependence. If children arrive, more growth is demanded. Those children will need adults as parents, not darling little girls or fathers afflicted with the Peter Pan Syndrome.

Many women grew up in dysfunctional families where the roles of mother and child were reversed. Mother was alcoholic, depressed, or sick; Daughter cared for Mother, held Mother, comforted Mother, wiped her tears and cooked her meals. Cheated out of her childhood, daughter grew up and struggled with longings for childhood and the nurturing she lacked.

If you were such a daughter, you have no doubts about your capabilities and strength. You developed those qualities early on. But your needs for mothering (or fathering) are legitimate and real. Perhaps you wonder if you are even lovable.

A NURTURING GOD

God wants to meet these needs. He sometimes describes himself in the Bible in "motherly" images—a nourisher, protector, care-giver. He can hold you in his lap and embrace you in a way you wished for when you were a child.

God also uses people to compensate for the nurturing you missed. Find a few people older than yourself who can encourage you to express your needs.

Learn to parent yourself as you should have been parented. Join a support group for those from dysfunctional families. You can break the family cycle and become an adult mother to your children.

The world needs adult women who are more concerned with loving responsibly than they are with asking questions about their own lovableness. God's desire for you is maturity, not the game-playing, manipulation, coyness, and pouting of the Darling.

The need for love is not adequately fulfilled when we get stuck childishly trying to reassure ourselves of our lovableness. We end up self-centered and narcissistic, never quite satisfied with the love we do receive.

Living as an adult woman brings the rewards and satisfactions of adult loving. When we focus on what we can give, many of the "me" issues disappear. Drawing on the love in our relationship with God, our ideal parent, we can grow beyond cuteness into the challenges of real life.

11

...

Growing Up
in Your Love Life

There is hope in the sphere of love. You are not forever limited by the counterfeits or deficiencies of love that have influenced your childhood, adolescence, or adult life until now.

All are born with handicaps. None of us had a perfect gene pool from which to form our bodies. We have not grown up with perfect parents, attended perfect schools, or been blessed with perfect friends.

God understands this. Part of his plan for salvation is to give us the capacity to grow in love. The Bible is written with the assumption that we want to learn about love. It urges us on to maturity in love by illuminating Jesus example and the stories of God's love for us.

Jesus defined the identifying mark of his disciples: "By this shall all men know that you are my disciples; that you have love one to another" (John 13:35). First John

169

admonishes us to let love perfect us. The Apostle Paul prayed the Philippians would grow in their love—a love full of knowledge and insight.

A maturing Christian can spot counterfeits. She recognizes their appearance in her own attempts to love and when others relate to her in such ways. Her love is sourced in her relationship with the One who deeply loves her.

Responding to God's love for me is the first step toward loving others. Until I experience love, I cannot give it. Human love is always a less than perfect sample, always a little flawed. I must receive the love of God as my supply and source.

Because of the risks of love, many make the simple choice: *don't get emotionally involved!* It sounds wise. But this is a coward's choice. God does not mean for us to live a stoic life, devoid of feeling. The Bible does not condemn emotions, it teaches us how to channel them. With its emphasis on love, our feelings are put in proper perspective.

Jesus would never have said, "Watch out for emotional involvement. Stay objective." He not only allowed himself to feel, he allowed his feelings to show:

"When he saw the crowds, he had compassion on them, because they were harassed and helpless, like sheep without a shepherd" (Matt. 9:36).

"When Jesus landed and saw a large crowd, he had compassion on them and healed their sick" (Matt. 14:15).

"Jesus had compassion on them and touched their eyes. Immediately they received their sight and followed him" (Matt. 20:34).

"As he approached Jerusalem and saw the city, he wept over it and said, "If you, even you, had only known on this day what would bring you peace" (Luke 19:41).

"When Jesus saw her weeping, and the Jews who had come along with her also weeping, he was deeply moved in spirit and troubled. 'Where have you laid him?' he asked. 'Come and see, Lord,' they replied. Jesus wept. Then the Jews said, 'See how he loved him!' " (John 11:33-36).

Forbidding ourselves emotional involvement is a self-protective sin. What we can forbid, instead, is the wrong ways of meeting our needs and falsely labeling it love. Our needs are valid. But our unhealthy ways of meeting them only serve to make us more needy.

"I'll just let God take care of my needs," one woman says. "He knows what they are and he's my healer."

Right! But not the whole story. The "healee" has a part to play. She is not a machine with a broken part. God doesn't rush to magically fix his robots so that he can quickly get them back into production. A woman is a living, conscious person, made in the image of God. God places great emphasis on understanding, clear thinking, and responsible choosing.

Most of us feel the need not only to receive love but to give it. We are often painfully aware of our lacks and failures in love. To change our patterns of "loving," we must see that our notion of what it means to love has gone ascrew. Owning the truth is half the battle. The other half involves a deep look inside to face the needs we have sought to meet in our counterfeit way of loving.

To understand a need is to relieve some of the desperation and mystery. We begin to make conscious choices about how we will address that need. We begin the upward climb out of the mysterious unknown. Understanding, says scripture, is essential. Following are just a few of the many passages that emphasize the importance of understanding:

"Cry aloud for understanding. . . . Then you will understand the fear of the Lord and find the knowledge of God. For the Lord gives wisdom, and from his mouth come knowledge and understanding" (Prov. 2:2-3, 5-6).

"I gain understanding from your precepts; therefore I hate every wrong path. Your word is a lamp to my feet and a light for my path" (Ps. 119:104-105).

"The unfolding of your words gives light; it gives understanding to the simple" (Ps. 119:130).

"Then you will understand what is right and just and fair—every good path. For wisdom will enter your heart, and knowledge will be pleasant to your soul. Discretion will protect you, and understanding will guard you" (Prov. 2:9-11).

"Get wisdom, get understanding.... Do not forsake wisdom, and she will protect you; love her, and she will watch over you" (Prov. 4:5-6).

"You who are simple, gain prudence; you who are foolish, gain understanding" (Prov. 8:5).

"Leave your simple ways and you will live; walk in the way of understanding" (Prov. 9:6).

"Blessed is the man who finds wisdom, the man who gains understanding, for she is more profitable than silver and yields better returns than gold. She is more precious than rubies; nothing you desire can compare with her" (Prov. 3:13-15).

God works patiently and tenderly *with* his creatures, never violating the delicate qualities that distinguish us from the animals: rational thinking and choice. God seldom uses a magic zap to heal us emotionally. *We* want it that way. More often, God leads us into health, never moving faster than we are able to respond.

SEEKING MATURE LOVE

The seeker of love must be an earnest seeker after wisdom, truth and understanding. Here are the ways we pray when we honestly wish to grow in our ability to love:

172

"Let me understand the teaching of your precepts; then I will meditate on your wonders" (Ps. 119:27).

"Keep me from deceitful ways; be gracious to me through your law. I have chosen the way of truth; I have set my heart on your laws" (Ps. 119:29-30).

"Teach me, O Lord, to follow your decrees; then I will keep them to the end. Give me understanding, and I will keep your law and obey it with all my heart. Direct me in the path of your commands, for there I find delight" (Ps. 119:33-35).

Seeking wisdom and understanding from God will lead us away from self-deception, rationalization, and other false means of coping with problems in our love relationships. We will choose to grow rather than remain hung-up on our particular need.

Professionals in the field of emotional health have long recognized a marked difference in the love that issues from a "growth-motivated" person as compared to a "deficiency-motivated" person:

> Growth-motivated and deficiency-motivated individuals have different types of interpersonal relations. The growth-motivated person is less dependent, less beholden to others, less needful of others' praise and affection, less anxious for honors, prestige, and rewards. He or she does not require continual interpersonal need gratification and, in fact, may at times feel hampered by others and prefer periods of privacy. Consequently the growth-motivated individual does not relate to others as *sources of supply* but is able to view them as complex, unique, whole beings. The deficiency-motivated individual, on the other hand, relates to others from the point of view of usefulness. Those aspects of the other that are not related to the

perceiver's needs are either overlooked altogether or regarded as an irritant or a threat. Thus, love is transformed into something else and resembles our relationships "with cows, horses, and sheep . . . or others whom we use."[1]

An Associated Press story in the Bellevue Journal American on March 9, 1989, illustrates "growth-motivated" love:

YAKIMA, WA (AP) — A retired nurse left Friday for Michigan to offer her services free of charge to a couple struggling to raise a new set of quintuplets and three other children.

Betty Clark, 64, said she heard about the plight of Michele and Ray L'Esperance, of Clarkston, Michigan, through magazines and television and decided to help.

"They looked like they'd been hit over the head," Clark, who is the mother of six, said Thursday.

"I was watching too much television anyway," said the former head nurse of the neonatal intensive care unit at Yakima Valley Memorial Hospital. "This retirement isn't for me."

"Besides, I'm only almost 65 and I've got a lot of energy. And I've never been to Detroit."

The quintuplets, four boys and a girl, were born January 11. They are the first quints conceived in vitro and born in the United States.

Earlier this week, the L'Esperances said they would allow their babies to be used in commercials because they couldn't make ends meet on Ray's annual salary of $26,000 as a corrections officer.

The babies go through 60 to 70 diapers a day, and a

routine visit to the doctor costs $300.

Clark, with 44 years of nursing experience, is offering her services as nurse, cook and babysitter for as long as they need her.

She sent a letter to the family offering to help several weeks ago and got a call from Michele L'Esperance about two weeks ago, she said.

"She said they were cautious about any offers and had checked my credentials," Clark said. "Apparently I got good reviews, because then she asked "When can you come?"

Clark's children have all left home, and she is no longer married. She has relatives to care for her Yakima home.

"There's nothing keeping me here at all," she said.

Clark said she was more concerned about the harried young couple, and their marriage, than the infants.

"You could see in the magazine stories what was happening," Clark said. "Those two are being pushed to the brink. I've counseled hundreds of parents over the years, and in each case like this it's important that the bonding between those two continues, that they somehow survive all this."

"They have to have time by themselves, for themselves," she said.

Years of handling newborns will make working with the quintuplets "easy," Clark said.

"I'll show them how to take care of their babies by doing it," she said.

Clark insists she has no motive except to help the family.

"I'm too young to retire," she said.

Many people marry out of "deficiency-motivated love" only to find marriage doesn't meet all their needs. After a few years, they say, "I don't love you anymore!" It would be more accurate to say, "You are not meeting my needs."

For instance, take the need for intimacy. Intimacy is not equivalent to love. Feelings of intimacy should not necessarily be labeled love. We all have a deep need for others to understand and listen to us. We instinctively desire to be visible to at least one other person. Visibility is the experience of being seen or known to someone; another person cares enough about me to allow me to reveal myself.

But visibility can be deceiving. Every person gifted with the ability to make me feel visible is not a person who loves me. Although the feelings visibility brings meet a genuine emotional need, don't mistake them for love. When two people are committed to an interdependent partnership, the lack of visibility can be remedied.

In that commitment, both parties are interested in meeting each other's needs and allow each other the freedom to express those needs. Blaming, accusations, judgments, and "if you really loved me" statements hinder intimacy. Instead, use the direct statement, "I'm feeling a need for . . ." with no demands attached.

No husband can meet all his wife's needs. Or vice versa. We didn't marry to have a supply depot—a need-filling warehouse.

Most couples who complain of a lack of intimacy are surprised to discover how many needs are met by simply becoming sounding boards for each other. Tension is released when we describe our troublesome emotions to a caring person. Verbal expression causes the feeling to come into focus, and it becomes much less intense, much less frightening.

Jerry and I call this spilling of emotions "R & R."

176

"R & R" stands for "rant and rave." When I tell him I need some R & R, he agrees to listen to my feelings without judgement, even if they sound like the carryings on of a raving maniac. We find that a drive is a safe place to do this, particularly if the children have precipitated my insane emotions!

I can also be a safe sounding board for Jerry if I put aside any obligation to "solve the problem" or censor his feelings. I had to learn to *not* say "You shouldn't feel that way!" Instead, I try to see the situation through his eyes, and identify with his feelings.

I haven't always understood these things. I used to sabotage intimacy and blame my husband for the lack of it. I wished for more intimacy and worked against it. I wasn't a safe place for Jerry to express his emotions. I wanted him to feel *only* the emotions with which I was comfortable: happiness, joy, compassion, admiration, courage, and tenderness—things like that.

In retrospect, I can understand people who believe their marriage is lonely and incapable of providing satisfaction. I had to become comfortable admitting and owning my own emotions before I could perceive my mistakes. Many give up hope too soon because they don't see that a different concept of marriage and a different way of relating will change things.

Even the best marriages have times when needs are not met, times when imbalances of give and take occur. The Christian concept of marriage takes those times into account. It provides a secure framework in which these challenges to love are met successfully.

THE CHRISTIAN MARRIAGE COMMITMENT

An engaged man in his mid-thirties asked me about Christian marriage. "How can I be sure I'll love her all my life? What if I wake up one morning five years from now and find I've fallen out of love?"

Marriage is a *choice* to love one person permanently. It is not based on how I feel but on what I commit myself to *do*. I cannot promise any person that I will feel warm emotions toward him each second of each twenty-four hour day for the next seventy years! How could any of us make such a promise? Who is foolish enough to believe her emotions are that controllable—or that predictable? Christians believe in a basis for marriage which is more secure than that.

I cannot commit myself to feel certain emotions for you at all times, but I can commit myself to act for your good and care about you and your well being. I can decide I will "do you good and not evil all the days of my life," as was said of the strong and lovely woman of Proverbs 31. I can commit myself to loving you for yourself.

Famous thinkers like Abraham Maslow, Erich Fromm, and Martin Buber have studied love as a psychological phenomenon, each coming from different assumptions about man, the world, and God. They all arrive, however, at a definition of mature, healthy love that sounds remarkably like 1 Corinthians 13. Although the Bible does not use psychological jargon and was written long before the science of psychology existed, it offers a more substantial and clear-cut way of understanding love than is found in any other piece of literature. In earliest times, even before God demonstrated the full extent of his love through Jesus Christ, Old Testament pages of scripture revealed it.

THE BIBLE'S CONCEPT OF LOVE

"Love your neighbor as yourself" (Matt. 22:39). Certainly this is one of the most familiar statements about love in the Bible. Almost anyone can quote it, even those who have never opened a Bible. We must understand this verse in its context, however, if we are to comprehend a biblical concept of love. Jesus spoke those famous words in answer to a question.

Hearing that Jesus had silenced the Sadducees, the Pharisees got together. One of them, an expert in the law, tested him with this question: "Teacher, which is the greatest commandment in the Law?"
Jesus replied: "Love the Lord your God with all your heart and with all your soul and with all your mind. This is the first and greatest commandment. And the second is like it: Love your neighbor as yourself. All the Law and the Prophets hang on these two commandments" (Matt. 22:34-40).

The subject under discussion was the Law of Moses, specifically, the Ten Commandments. Jesus quoted from the Jewish law just as the Pharisees expected. "Thou shalt love the Lord your God with all your heart and with all your soul and with all your mind." Jesus declared this one as the greatest commandment.

Then he added a second commandment that he said was *like the first.* But the second commandment was not from the list. It didn't appear in the ten at all; in fact, it wasn't even number eleven. However, Jesus was quoting from the Books of the Law, and his questioners no doubt were familiar with Leviticus 19 where it appears.

When you read Leviticus 19, several things become clear; ideas about love well-known in Jesus' day but foggy in ours. We have so emotionalized the word that we've lost the simple meaning of love as people in earlier centuries understood it. Look at where and how this statement was first made:

Do not defraud your neighbor or rob him.

Do not hold back the wages of a hired man overnight.

Do not curse the deaf or put a stumbling block in front of the blind, but fear your God. I am the Lord.

Do not pervert justice; do not show partiality to the poor or favoritism to the great, but judge your neighbor fairly.

Do not go about spreading slander among your people.

Do not do anything that endangers your neighbor's life. I am the Lord.

Do not hate your brother in your heart. Rebuke your neighbor frankly so you will not share in his guilt.

Do not seek revenge or bear a grudge against one of your people, but *love your neighbor as yourself* (Lev. 19:13-18).

Here is a list of cruel, deceitful, and selfish things people do to each other. God is specific; no generalities here. No, "don't treat other people badly; you know what I mean." God intends for us to value other human beings in the same way we value ourselves. He wants us to acknowledge the value he places on that other person. Twice the statement is added, "I am the Lord"—as though humans need to remember God in heaven sees when they violate one of his children.

Belief in and respect for God is the basis of any workable system of ethics. Human philosophies, tastes, and preferences will only help us rationalize what we want to do. For example, "We were in love; we had to do it." Or "It can't be wrong because it feels so right."

Because the human heart can be deceptive, fooling even

its owner, we all need someone wiser than ourselves to define what love does and does not do. God clearly spelled out the definitions in the Bible. We have an objective standard.

Something else is interesting about the preceding list: it is a list of choices. None of these things just happens; I have to choose to do them. We don't "accidentally" rob someone, show partiality to a rich person, or make a blind man fall down.

LOVE: THE ALTERNATIVE CHOICE

The alternative choice to all these forbidden behaviors is the choice to love. Like a dichotomy of good and evil, you can either treat others in despicable, unfair ways, or you can love them. If you choose to value others with the same value you place on yourself, you'll treat them well. This assumes, of course, that you value yourself as God values you. Self-hatred is a lack of trust in God and of believing that he values you. Devaluing yourself is never an act of love.

When speaking of love, the Bible doesn't mention emotions, except "hating your brother in your heart." It doesn't demand you have warm "feelings" toward your neighbor. It simply insists, without qualification, that you make the choice to love him or her. Love is not the way you feel. It's the way you treat another person. You don't have to be "in love" to treat another human being with respect, honesty, fairness, and kindness. You simply make a decision: I choose to treat you as you should be treated.

The only place that loving your neighbor as yourself is even mentioned in the Old Testament is in Leviticus. But it appears many times in the New Testament. Since Jesus stressed it so often, and went on to explain that love fulfills all the other commandments, the early Christian leaders majored on the subject of loving our neighbor.

James called it the royal law of love. Paul wrote that we are set free from the law to "serve one another in love," and John penned a whole book about it, concluding that anyone who truly loves God *will* love others. He concluded that it is impossible to know God and continue to live in an unloving fashion. The seed of God's life in us will inevitably bear fruit and that fruit is love.

Even enemies are included in God's command to love. In Old Testament times it was normal to hate your enemies. But Jesus said his followers would have a new ethic; they would even love their enemies. He didn't mean that they would feel warm sentimental feelings. He meant that they would give up their desire to pay back hatred and revenge.

In fact, they would surrender inner hatred and vengeful plans—they would return to the ancient command that restores truth and trust to strained relationships: honest communication.

If I do not hate my brother in my heart, but instead rebuke him frankly, then I will not get to the point of bearing a grudge or seeking revenge (Lev. 19:17-18). Imagine all the suffering this world could have been spared if the original hearers had practiced Leviticus 19! Honest communication is essential to love.

Truth is listed in 1 Corinthians 13 as essential to love, as we have repeatedly pointed out in this book. Only when truth is present can trust exist in a relationship. Love does not operate in a framework of deception, mask-wearing, role-playing, manipulation, and mind games. Hidden agendas, secret expectations, possessiveness, and desires to control are all enemies of love.

Agape love is not an exclusive love for one person that reduces relationships with all others to insignificance.

Rather, *agape* love is a life attitude, an environment you carry within yourself. A woman who loves only one person has not yet experienced *agape*.

Agape love reaches out and includes rather than drawing into oneself. When *agape* is channeled into friendship, it does not grasp one "best friend" and ignore all others. When expressed in parenting, it does not use the child as an object of gratification. When expressed in a romantic relationship, *agape* is a giving spirit, delighting in truth and the well-being of its object.

Agape is "being love" and "growth-motivated love." It loves the *being* of another rather than the satisfaction the other can produce. It is sourced in my growth rather than in my needs and deficits. *Agape* love is not a means to an end; it is an end in itself. Love is its own reward.

J.B. Phillips' paraphrase of the love chapter sums it up:

You should set your hearts on the best spiritual gifts, but I shall show a way which surpasses them all. If I speak with the eloquence of men and of angels, but have no love, I become no more than blaring brass or crashing cymbal. If I have the gift of foretelling the future and hold in my mind not only all human knowledge but the very secrets of God, and if I also have that absolute faith which can move mountains, but have no love, I amount to nothing at all. If I dispose of all that I possess, yes, even if I give my own body to be burned, but have no love, I achieve precisely nothing.

This love of which I speak is slow to lose patience—it looks for a way of being constructive. It is not possessive: it is neither anxious to impress nor does it cherish inflated ideas of its own importance.

Love has good manners and does not pursue selfish

advantage. It is not touchy. It does not keep account of evil or gloat over the wickedness of other people. On the contrary, it is glad with all good men when truth prevails.

Love knows no limit to its endurance, no end to its trust, no fading of its hope; it can outlast anything. It is, in fact, the one thing that still stands when all else has fallen.

For if there are prophecies they will be fulfilled and done with, if there are "tongues" the need for them will disappear, if there is knowledge it will be swallowed up in truth. For our knowledge is always incomplete and our prophecy is always incomplete, and when the complete comes, that is the end of the incomplete.

When I was a little child I talked and felt and thought like a little child. Now that I am a man my childish speech and feeling and thought have no further significance for me.

At present we are men looking at puzzling reflections in a mirror. The time will come when we shall see reality whole and face to face! At present all I know is a little fraction of the truth, but the time will come when I shall know it as fully as God now knows me!

In this life we have three great lasting qualities—faith, hope and love. But the greatest of them is love.[2]

Source Notes and Suggested Reading

CHAPTER ONE

1. Leo Buscaglia, *Bus 9 to Paradise*, (New York, NY: Ballantine Books, a division of Random House, Inc., 1986), p. 21.

SUGGESTED SCRIPTURE PASSAGES ABOUT LOVE

1 John
Hosea
1 Corinthians 13
Leviticus 19:18
Romans 12
Ephesians 3:17-19

Luke 10:25-37
James 2:8
Galatians 5:13-26
Romans 13:8-10, 20
Philippians 1:9-11

CHAPTER THREE

1. Robin Norwood, *Women Who Love Too Much* (New York, NY: Simon & Schuster, 1985), p. 152.
2. *Women Who Love Too Much*, p. 152.
3. Carl Rogers, *Becoming Partners* (New York, NY: Dell Publishing Company, 1972), pp. 25-26.
4. *Becoming Partners*, p. 26.

RESOURCE READING FOR RESCUERS

Neff, Pauline. *Tough Love: How Parents Can Deal With Drug Abuse*. Nashville, TN: Abingdon, 1982.

A book for parents whose children are now on drugs or are exposed to drug users, with the author's proposal for a cure for drug abusers and positive support for their families.

Strom, Kay Marshall. *Helping Women in Crisis*. Grand Rapids, MI: Zondervan, 1986.

This is a handbook for people-helpers. It will help you channel all those good rescuing energies into effective ministy. Practical how-to training to provide you with the skills and knowledge needed to do the right thing at the right time.

TO HELP SOMEONE ADDICTED TO ALCOHOL OR DRUGS

Al-Anon has a number of books and pamphlets available. Some of the titles are *Living With An Alcoholic, The Dilemma of the Alcoholic Marriage, One Day at a Time in Al-Anon.*

For a complete literature catalog and price list write:

Al-Anon Family Group Headquarters

P.O. Box 183, Madison Square Garden
New York, NY 10017

Help for the Alcoholic is a ninety-minute cassette tape available from:

Focus on the Family
Box 500
Arcadia, CA 91006

Many tools are available. Here are just a few:

Hotline. A national drug and alcohol abuse hotline can be reached by calling this toll-free number: 1-800-BE-SO-BER.

Al-Anon. This is a support group for families who have to cope with an alcoholic relative. Associated with Alcoholics Anonymous, it also has chapters all over the country. Their headquarters are at:

Al-Anon Family Group Headquarters
P.O. Box 183, Madison Square Garden
New York, NY 10017

Alateen. This is the teenage division of Al-Anon. It is specifically intended for young people with alcoholic parents. Its headquarters has the same address as Al-Anon.

National Clearinghouse for Alcohol Information. This organization offers a number of free services and products. It provides referrals on request as well as directories of treatment resources for each of the fifty states. It can be contacted at:

P.O. Box 2345
Rockville, MD 20852
Telephone: (301) 468-2600

CHAPTER FOUR

1. Patricia Campbell Hearst with Alvin Moscow, *Patty Hearst* (New York, NY: Avon Books, 1982).
2. Ann Rule, *The Stranger Beside Me* (New York, NY: W.W. Norton & Company Inc., 1980), p. 354.
3. *The Stranger Beside Me*, p. 398.

RESOURCE READING FOR VICTIMS

Black, Claudia. *It Will Never Happen to Me.* New York, NY: Ballantine Books, 1981.

This is a touching, encouraging book for those who grew up in a home where alcoholism existed. Twenty-eight million Americans are children of alcoholics. Many of them find themselves in victim roles as adults. With understanding and help, that can be changed. An Adult Children of Alcoholics group may also be beneficial to you—check to see if one meets in your church.

Cook, Barbara. *Ordinary Women, Extraordinary Strength.* Lynnwood, WA: Aglow Publications, 1988.

This book was meant to give women spiritual backbone; security in their knowledge of their own worth, value, identity, and power—qualities essential to a woman who needs to change from a victim status to one of freedom and wholeness.

Forward, Dr. Susan. *Men Who Hate Women (And the Women Who Love Them).* New York, NY: Bantam Books, 1986.

All victims are not necessarily mistreated by "men who hate women." However, this book shares good insights and offers many practical helps.

Norwood, Robin. *Women Who Love Too Much*. New York, NY: Simon & Schuster, 1985.

Olson, Esther Lee and Kenneth Peterson. *No Place To Hide*. Wheaton, IL: Tyndale House, 1983.
One out of every two wives in America has been abused by her husband. Four to five million have been injured badly. According to studies, the majority of these women come from "middle-class and higher-income homes, where the power of money is held by the men."
Many are evangelical Christian women, including wives of pastors and church leaders. Written by a Christian counselor, this true story is helpful for an abused woman who wonders what she ought to do next.

Vredevelt, Pamela and Kathy Rodriguez. *Surviving the Secret*. Old Tappan, NJ: Fleming Revell, 1987.
If your "victim role" has its roots in childhood sexual abuse, this book will help you understand many of your feelings and habits. Two Christian counselors explain how you may have been affected. They also provide concrete steps which will lead to your healing and future happiness, along with valuable scripture passages applying to your needs and questions.

CHAPTER SIX

1. Dr. Connell Cowan and Dr. Melvyn Kinder, *Smart Women, Foolish Choices* (New York, NY: Clarkson N. Potter, Inc., 1985), p. 176.
2. Carol Cassell, *Swept Away* (New York, NY: Simon & Schuster, 1984), p. 5.
3. *Swept Away*, p. 4.

4. John Powell, *Unconditional Love* (Niles, IL: Argus Communications, 1978), p. 50.
5. Daniel Goldstine, Katherine Larner, Shirley Zuckerman, and Hilary Goldstine, *The Dance-Away Lover* (New York, NY: Wm. Morrow and Co., 1977), p. 163.
6. *The Dance-Away Lover*, pp. 164-167.
7. *The Dance-Away Lover*, p. 187.
8. Barbara Cook, *Romantic Love* (Kirkland, WA: Eastside Church), audiotape. (To order this tape or receive information about all Marriage Enrichment Seminar Tapes, contact: RESOURCE, P.O. Box 536, Kirkland, WA 98083-9910 or phone (206) 823-2033.)

CHAPTER SEVEN

1. Jerry Cook and Stanley Baldwin, *A Few Things I Learned Since I Knew It All* (Irving, TX: Word Books, Inc.), 1989, pp. 9-11.
2. Dr. Kevin Leman, *The Pleasers* (Old Tappan, NJ: Fleming H. Revell Co.), 1987, pp. 6-9.
3. *The Pleasers*, p. 9.
4. Collette Dowling, *Perfect Women* (New York, NY: Summit Books, a trademark of Simon & Schuster Inc.), 1988, pp. 133-134.
5. Barbara Cook, *Ordinary Women, Extraordinary Strength* (Lynnwood, WA: Aglow Publications), 1988, pp. 185, 190.

RESOURCE READING FOR THE ANGEL

Cook, Jerry and Stanley Baldwin. *A Few Things I've Learned Since I Knew It All*. Irving, TX: Word Books, 1989.

Jerry talks of the burnout and tiredness that take over the lives of many who minister constantly; he shares his own discoveries into a longer and simpler life.

Fezler, Dr. William and Eleanor S. Field. *The Good Girl Syndrome*. New York, NY: Macmillan Publishing Company, 1985.

The first page says it this way:

HELP WANTED: Martyr

JOB DESCRIPTION: Cater to the needs of everyone but yourself. Sacrifice career, achievement, independence, identity.

REWARD: Be called "virtuous," "an angel," "my sainted mother."

SALARY: Meager.

FRINGE BENEFITS: Anger. Unhappiness. Powerlessness.

This secular book contains helpful insights and suggestions.

Leman, Dr. Kevin. *The Pleasers*. Old Tappan, NJ: Fleming H. Revell Co., 1987.

Here is the book with the thorough, practical steps needed to change yourself into what Dr. Leman calls the "positive pleaser." For the woman who feels overwhelmed by work, home, or family, who feels manipulated, cheated, or abused, he offers step-by-step guidance to taking charge of your life, including how to deal with a controlling husband. Explains how to know the difference between being assertive and aggressive, discusses how to please yourself without feeling guilty, develop a positive self-image, get out of the "controller swamp," and other issues.

CHAPTER EIGHT

1. Pamela Vredevelt and Kathryn Rodriguez, *Surviving the Secret* (Old Tappan, NJ: Fleming H. Revell Co., 1987), p. 37.
2. *Surviving the Secret*, pp. 189-190.
3. *Surviving the Secret*, pp. 190-191.
4. Patrick Carnes, Ph.D., *Out of the Shadows* (Minneapolis, MN: Compcare Publications, 1983), p. vii.

RESOURCE READING FOR THE ADDICT

Armstrong, Louise. *Kiss Daddy Goodnight*. New York, NY: Hawthorn Books, 1978.

Bass, E. and Thornton L. Bass, ed. *I Never Told Anyone: Writings By Women Survivors*. New York, NY: Harper & Row, 1983.

Carnes, Dr. Patrick. *Out of the Shadows*. Minneapolis, MN: Compcare Publications, 1983.
If you suspect addict tendencies in yourself or someone close to you, this should be the first book you turn to. Dr. Carnes explains how addicts are treated without disrupting their jobs and families.
You will learn the next steps to take, whether you or another is addicted.

Dobson, Dr. James. *Love Must Be Tough*. Waco, TX: Word Books, 1983.
This book stresses the idea of forcing an unfaithful partner to accept the responsibility for his actions.

Edwards, Katherine. *A House Divided*. Grand Rapids, MI: Zondervan, 1985.

The autobiography of an incest victim who is a former missionary. Also contains information on how to report incest, and lists agencies for legal, financial, and emotional aid.

Hyde, Margaret O. *Sexual Abuse, Let's Talk About It.* Philadelphia, PA: Westminster, 1985.
Includes a list by state of concerned organizations. For ages ten and older.

Kuhne, Karen. *A Healing Season.* Grand Rapids, MI: Zondervan, 1985.
This is an autobiography of an unfaithful Christian and her reconciliation with her husband.

Lutzer, Erwin. *Living With Your Passions.* Wheaton, IL: Victor Books, 1983.
A how-to book useful for individual reading or for group study. A leader's guide is available.

Vredevelt, Pamela and Kathryn Rodriguez. *Surviving the Secret.* Old Tappan, NJ: Fleming H. Revell Co., 1987.
Two Christian counselors share in plain language how you can receive healing from incest or childhood sexual abuse even if you were denied help years ago or immediately following the incident. They tell the stories of women abused in Christian homes, plus success stories of women who overcame the effects of incest and found fulfilling lives.

The following organizations provide help for the victim of incest:

V.O.I.C.E. (Victims of Incest Can Emerge)
Grand Junction, CO 81501
(303) 241-2746

Child Help USA
Woodland Hills, CA 91370
1-800-4-A-CHILD

Child Sexual Abuse Treatment Program
467 S. Third Street
San Jose, CA 95110

National Center for the Prevention of Child Abuse and
Neglect
P.O. Box 1182
Washington, D.C. 20013
(202) 245-2856

CHAPTER NINE

1. Dr. Connell Cowan and Dr. Melvyn Kinder, *Smart Women, Foolish Choices* (New York, NY: Clarkson N. Potter, Inc.), 1985, pp. 155-160.
2. *Smart Women, Foolish Choices*, p. 161.

RESOURCE READING FOR THE OBSESSED

Colgrove, Melba, Ph.D., Harold H. Bloomfield, M.D., and Peter McWilliams. *How To Survive the Loss of a Love.* Allen Park, MI: Leo Press Inc., 1976.
    This is my personal preference of all the books written about grief. It's small, compassionate, and designed to guide you through the grief process in a way that will bring you not only healing but genuine growth.

Cowan, Dr. Connell and Dr. Melvyn Kinder. *Smart Women, Foolish Choices.* New York, NY: Clarkson N. Potter, Inc., 1985.
You can probably read this little book in one sitting. It points out the difference between love and longing. Chapter 8 is especially pertinent. Entitled "Release From Endless Mourning," it has sections subtitled "Believing In Magic," "Wounded Self-Esteem," and "Release to Love Again."

Halpern, Howard M. *How to Break Your Addiction to a Person.* New York, NY: McGraw Hill Inc., 1982.
This book provides the support you need to break the addiction to a person. It is about when love doesn't work, including, "When you don't know whether to continue a relationship," "When you know you should let go and don't," "When you believe you can't live without that person," and "When you think you will never find somebody else again."

Norwood, Robin. *Women Who Love Too Much.* New York, NY: Simon & Schuster, Inc., 1985.
This book contains many stories of women who mistook obsession for love. Helps you get in touch with the factors in your background related to obsessive relationships; how your childhood experiences with love may have left you confused; when love involves pain, longing, or suffering, etc.

CHAPTER TEN

1. Elizabeth Rice Handford, *Me? Obey Him?* (Murfreesboro, TN: Sword of the Lord Publishers), 1972, p. 67.

2. *Me? Obey Him?*, p. 67.
3. *Me? Obey Him?*, p. 68.
4. Helen Andelin, *Fascinating Womanhood*, (Santa Barbara, CA: Pacific Press), 1965.
5. Dr. Connell Cowan and Dr. Melvyn Kinder, *Smart Women, Foolish Choices* (New York, NY: Clarkson N. Potter, Inc.) 1985, pp. 30-31.
6. *Smart Women, Foolish Choices*, pp. 31-32.
7. *Smart Women, Foolish Choices*, pp. 33-35.

RESOURCE READING FOR THE DARLING

Cook, Barbara. *Ordinary Women, Extraordinary Strength.* Lynnwood, WA: Aglow Publications, 1988.
This was written for women who feel ambivalent about their own strength and afraid of being unfeminine if they are strong. A full treatment of what the Bible says on these issues.

Cowan, Dr. Connell and Dr. Melvyn Kinder. *Smart Women, Foolish Choices.* New York, NY: Clarkson N. Potter, Inc., 1985.
I would suggest two chapters especially. One is entitled "Daddy's Little Girl," which deals with "Learning to be Cute," "Learning to be Indirect," the "Powerful Father," the "Missing Father," the "Unresponsive Father," and the "Secret Need to be Rescued." The second is chapter 3, "How Men Respond to Daddy's Little Girl."

Missildine, W. H. *Your Inner Child of the Past.* New York, NY: Simon & Schuster, 1963.
The most valuable book I can suggest to anyone who struggles with unresolved issues from childhood. Helpful to the self-punishing and perfectionistic as well as to the

self-indulgent. Recognizes that we tend to treat ourselves in the familiar patterns we saw in our parents, even when those patterns are recognized as unfair or harmful.

CHAPTER ELEVEN

1. Irvin D. Yalom, *Existential Psychotherapy* (New York, NY: Basic Books, Inc.), 1980, p. 369.
2. J. B. Phillips, translation, *The New Testament in Modern English* (New York, NY: The Macmillan Company), 1962, pp. 370-371.

Inquiries regarding speaking availability and other correspondence may be directed to Barbara Cook at the following address:

Eastside Church
P.O. Box 536
Kirkland, WA 98083-0536